Troubleshooting CentOS

A practical guide to troubleshooting the CentOS 7
community-based enterprise server

Jonathan Hobson

BIRMINGHAM - MUMBAI

Troubleshooting CentOS

First published: June 2015

Production reference: 1220615

Published by Packt Publishing Ltd.
Livery Place
35 Livery Street
Birmingham B3 2PB, UK.

ISBN 978-1-78528-982-8

www.packtpub.com

Credits

Author
Jonathan Hobson

Reviewers
Mohamed Alibi

Toni de la Fuente

Commissioning Editor
Neil Alexander

Acquisition Editor
Usha Iyer

Content Development Editor
Anand Singh

Technical Editors
Dhiraj Chandanshive

Pramod Kumavat

Copy Editors
Janbal Dharmaraj

Rashmi Sawant

Project Coordinator
Vijay Kushlani

Proofreader
Safis Editing

Indexer
Hemangini Bari

Production Coordinator
Shantanu N. Zagade

Cover Work
Shantanu N. Zagade

About the Author

Jonathan Hobson is a professional Dev/Ops engineer who provides round-the-clock application and server support to one of the world's largest online newspapers. He has been using CentOS since its inception, and as the author of the best-selling *CentOS 6 Linux Server Cookbook, Packt Publishing* (ISBN-13: 978-1849519021), Jonathan maintains a strong reputation for the generation of ideas, problem solving, building business confidence, and finding innovative solutions in challenging environments.

Jonathan has worked in a variety of environments, and with more than 20 years of experience as a professional developer, database administrator, and server engineer, he continues to support the open source community at large.

Following a wide range of interests beyond the computer screen, Jonathan also enjoys walking his dogs and getting out and about in the great outdoors.

This book is dedicated to those I love and the things I have achieved. A new story has just begun.

About the Reviewers

Mohamed Alibi is a system and network administrator for bioinformatics research computer infrastructure at the Institut Pasteur de Tunis. He received his master's degree diploma in network system and telecommunication from the Faculty of Sciences, Tunis El-Manar. His did his master's graduation internship at the University of Illinois at Urbana-Champaign (United States) from the National Center for Supercomputing Applications and the Institution for Genomic Biology, where he helped develop and adapt a data transfer solution to be used in bioinformatics research centers across Africa.

He started his career in 2011 as a technical support assistant and was promoted in 2012. He is currently part of a network project called H3ABioNet that helps African nodes enhance their bio-informatics research capacities. He was the co-chair of the Infrastructure Working Group, a group that helps to develop and enhance the computer infrastructure of project nodes. Since 2015, he has been training at the technical workshops held at the University of Pretoria (South Africa) as a system administrator of the African Nodes. Since 2014, he has also been a computer science professor at the Higher Institute of Biotechnology of Sidi Thabet.

I would like to acknowledge my family for their constant support and my friends and colleagues for helping me make better decisions. Finally, I would like to thank the H3ABioNet Consortium for giving me the opportunity to expand my knowledge and experience to be capable of doing this work.

Toni de la Fuente is the principal solutions engineer for the Americas at Alfresco. He is the author of *Backup and Disaster Recovery White Paper* and *Alfresco Security Best Practices*.

He has more than 17 years of experience in security architecture, systems administration, ECM architecture, cloud computing, and monitoring and scalability projects. He has a variety of certifications, such as the LPI Linux certification, Red Hat Certified Engineer (RHCE), ITIL v3, and an AWS Certified Solutions Architect. Recently, he did an advanced training course in computer forensics and is a collaborator to the UOC University.

Toni is a declared open source enthusiast and computer security lover, having founded phpRADmin, a security open source project in 2006 and Alfresco BART (a backup tool). He has participated in other open source-related projects, such as Madrid Wireless, Linux Fedora, OpenSolaris Hispano, and multiple Alfresco-related plugins, such as the Nagios plugin. His name is mentioned in different books on network security, among others. He regularly teaches, conducts lectures, courses, and conferences in events in Europe, the United States, and Latin America. He has also contributed to the world of open source for more than 13 years with his blog at http://byx.com and through Twitter at https://twitter.com/toniblyx.

This is the third book he has contributed to Packt Publishing. We also collaborated with him on *Building a Home Security System with BeagleBone* and *Icinga Network Monitoring*.

www.PacktPub.com

Support files, eBooks, discount offers, and more

For support files and downloads related to your book, please visit www.PacktPub.com.

Did you know that Packt offers eBook versions of every book published, with PDF and ePub files available? You can upgrade to the eBook version at www.PacktPub.com and as a print book customer, you are entitled to a discount on the eBook copy. Get in touch with us at service@packtpub.com for more details.

At www.PacktPub.com, you can also read a collection of free technical articles, sign up for a range of free newsletters and receive exclusive discounts and offers on Packt books and eBooks.

https://www2.packtpub.com/books/subscription/packtlib

Do you need instant solutions to your IT questions? PacktLib is Packt's online digital book library. Here, you can search, access, and read Packt's entire library of books.

Why subscribe?

- Fully searchable across every book published by Packt
- Copy and paste, print, and bookmark content
- On demand and accessible via a web browser

Free access for Packt account holders

If you have an account with Packt at www.PacktPub.com, you can use this to access PacktLib today and view 9 entirely free books. Simply use your login credentials for immediate access.

Table of Contents

Preface

CentOS (Community Enterprise Operating System) is known as a robust, stable, and generally trouble-free operating system that is particularly well-suited to the role of a server. As a faithful adaption of RHEL, CentOS has been with us since its initial release in May 2004. It is used by a significant number of servers across the world, by an increasing number of individuals and businesses for a variety of needs, and it can be found in many mission critical situations. CentOS is considered to be a favorite among Linux professionals, and if it is configured correctly, serviced, and maintained, in most instances, a CentOS-based server should never give rise to any major complications. However, there are occasions when things do go wrong, and in such a situation, where the old joke of "rebooting the machine" is not the most appropriate form of action, then your only recourse is to consider troubleshooting the system.

Based on the overall theme of troubleshooting a CentOS 7 server, the purpose of this book is to take you on a journey across the whole spectrum of issue-based problem solving. Active processes, the networking environment, package management, users, directories and files, shared resources, security, databases, web-based services, and DNS will all be encountered with the sole purpose of building your knowledge base and enabling you to develop a fresh approach to problem solving.

What this book covers

Chapter 1, Basics of Troubleshooting CentOS, serves as an introduction to the book, in general, by giving you the low-down on gathering hardware information, dmesg, working with log files, and learning how to manipulate these log files using an array of command-line tools.

Chapter 2, Troubleshooting Active Processes, takes up the running and dives into the world of tuning server performance, swap, memory management, system load, monitoring disk I/O, a tour of the system, guidance on issuing the kill signal, and running additional performance checks using many more tools associated with the command line.

Chapter 3, Troubleshooting the Network Environment, walks you through the process of diagnosing a variety of issues related to the network environment. ping, dig, host, traceroute, mtr, ss, and tcpdump are just some of the tools that will be discussed when highlighting a whole host of network-related problems.

Chapter 4, Troubleshooting Package Management and System Upgrades, puts yum (Yellowdog Updater, Modified) in the spotlight with the intention of showing you how to manage plugins, add additional repositories, download RPM packages, restore the RPM database, and gather generalized software information.

Chapter 5, Troubleshooting Users, Directories, and Files, takes a stance on on-going maintenance and provides the information you need to prepare you for a variety of issues that the professional troubleshooter may face. From user management to login.defs, utmpdump to general file and directory audits. This chapter also builds on your existing knowledge related to the XFS filesystem and shows you how to recover the lost data with Scalpel.

Chapter 6, Troubleshooting Shared Resources, takes a magnifying glass to NFS on CentOS 7 and shows you how to provide shares, manage exports, and access them via a client workstation while simultaneously approaching the subject of CIFS and autofs to deliver an all round problem solving guide.

Chapter 7, Troubleshooting Security Issues, builds on the momentum and discusses why you need to keep SELinux by showing you how to generate audit reports with aureport. From this point onward, you will discover a comprehensive review on FirewallD and an installation guide for Tripwire so that you can develop your very own intrusion detection system.

Chapter 8, Troubleshooting Database Services, lends a hand to troubleshooters and system administrators alike by taking the key points regarding MariaDB, MySQL, and PostgreSQL to provide a birds eye view of how to deal with a lost root password, database tuning, database metrics, and how to install MySQL server on CentOS 7.

Chapter 9, Troubleshooting Web Services, takes a step back from recovery and examines the need to improve a system, website, or web application. Taking you through the art of cURL, you will not only discover how to audit your server and access FTP, but you will also learn how to validate your Akamai headers and manage Varnish with the overall intention to illustrate the fine line between Dev/Ops and troubleshooting.

Chapter 10, Troubleshooting DNS Services, completes our journey with an investigation into a variety of domain name service issues. Hostnames, FQDNs, BIND, and iftop are all under the knife as we navigate to a number of issues related to bandwidth, cache flushing, and how to make a DNS health check.

What you need for this book

The requirement of this book is based on the use of CentOS 7, a community-supported distribution derived from sources freely provided to the public by Red Hat. As such, CentOS Linux is functionally compatible with RHEL (**Red Hat Enterprise Linux**), although some package names may have been changed in order to remove upstream vendor branding and artwork. CentOS Linux is available for free, at no cost, and free to redistribute.

Who this book is for

This is a practical guide used to troubleshoot the CentOS 7 community-based enterprise server. It is assumed that you already have a server up and running, a good working knowledge of CentOS, and that you are comfortable with the concept of working with the services used by your server. You are not expected to be an expert by any means, but the familiarity of working with a server by remote administration will always help.

Conventions

In this book, you will find a number of text styles that distinguish between different kinds of information. Here are some examples of these styles and an explanation of their meaning.

Code words in text, database table names, folder names, filenames, file extensions, pathnames, dummy URLs, user input, and Twitter handles are shown as follows: "Discover how to gather hardware-based system information using `lscpu` and `lspci`."

A block of code is set as follows:

```
/path/to/nfs/publication/directory
XXX.XXX.XXX.XXX(rw,sync,root_squash,no_all_squash)
```

Any command-line input or output is written as follows:

```
# yum groupinstall "Base" "Development Libraries" "Development Tools"
```

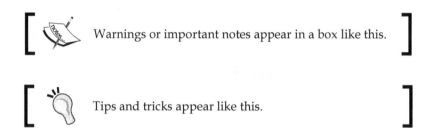

> Warnings or important notes appear in a box like this.

> Tips and tricks appear like this.

Reader feedback

Feedback from our readers is always welcome. Let us know what you think about this book—what you liked or disliked. Reader feedback is important for us as it helps us develop titles that you will really get the most out of.

To send us general feedback, simply e-mail feedback@packtpub.com, and mention the book's title in the subject of your message.

If there is a topic that you have expertise in and you are interested in either writing or contributing to a book, see our author guide at www.packtpub.com/authors.

Customer support

Now that you are the proud owner of a Packt book, we have a number of things to help you to get the most from your purchase.

Errata

Although we have taken every care to ensure the accuracy of our content, mistakes do happen. If you find a mistake in one of our books—maybe a mistake in the text or the code—we would be grateful if you could report this to us. By doing so, you can save other readers from frustration and help us improve subsequent versions of this book. If you find any errata, please report them by visiting http://www.packtpub.com/submit-errata, selecting your book, clicking on the **Errata Submission Form** link, and entering the details of your errata. Once your errata are verified, your submission will be accepted and the errata will be uploaded to our website or added to any list of existing errata under the Errata section of that title.

To view the previously submitted errata, go to https://www.packtpub.com/books/content/support and enter the name of the book in the search field. The required information will appear under the **Errata** section.

Piracy

Piracy of copyrighted material on the Internet is an ongoing problem across all media. At Packt, we take the protection of our copyright and licenses very seriously. If you come across any illegal copies of our works in any form on the Internet, please provide us with the location address or website name immediately so that we can pursue a remedy.

Please contact us at copyright@packtpub.com with a link to the suspected pirated material.

We appreciate your help in protecting our authors and our ability to bring you valuable content.

Questions

If you have a problem with any aspect of this book, you can contact us at questions@packtpub.com, and we will do our best to address the problem.

1
Basics of Troubleshooting CentOS

CentOS, the **Community Enterprise Operating System**, is known to be a robust, stable, and trouble-free platform that is particularly well suited to the role of a server. Used by organizations of all sizes, CentOS can be found in many mission-critical environments the world over. However, as servers are expected to work on demand and without interruption, there will be times when a calm but firm hand is required to restore a service or to make some final adjustments to an existing application in order to ensure that a "working state" can be resumed as quickly as possible:

"The server has gone down and all hell is about to break loose."

In a less than perfect world, things can (and inevitably do) go wrong, but it is your overall understanding of CentOS 7 and the confidence it provides that will form the basis of your troubleshooting skills. Remember, troubleshooting is a process of investigation that ultimately leads to a diagnosis. All systems are different and every approach to the same situation can vary depending on the purpose of that system. So, with this in mind, it is important to realize that the premise of this book is not recipe-driven, but more about the tools that are used and the resources you will be expected to encounter and interact with.

In this chapter, we will:

- Learn how to install some basic tools on CentOS
- Discover how to gather hardware-based system information using `lscpu` and `lspci`

- Learn more about the importance of dmesg and how it interacts with the kernel
- Learn about the more common log files and how they affect the log output
- Learn how to manipulate files of any description using grep, tail, cat, less, truncate, and many more command-line functions

Installing some basic tools

During the course of this book, it is assumed that you will already have access to the basic tools associated with troubleshooting your server. Some of the more obscure tools will be mentioned and instructions will be given; however, for those who may or may not have access to the basic toolbox, as the root user you may want to begin by running the following command:

```
# yum groupinstall "Base" "Development Libraries" "Development Tools"
```

This action, if and when confirmed, will begin to download and install the common development tools, libraries, and base components of a CentOS server system. It also contains the relevant utilities required by RPM, additional text editors, and packages required to compile custom packages.

> The practice of installing these packages at the outset is optional and all of these packages can be installed individually (as and when required). However, in an environment where disaster recovery planning has a vital role to play, it is worth considering the notion that a server has everything in place before any issues arise.

So, having prepared the system with the necessary tools and utilities, we shall begin in earnest by taking a closer look at the hardware. To do this, it is recommended that you continue with root access to the system in question.

Gathering hardware information

As a matter of principle, most people will tend to suggest that all system information can be categorized as either hardware-or-software based. This approach certainly serves to simplify things, but throughout the course of this chapter I will go some way to infer that there are instances in which the interplay of both (hardware and software) can be the reason for the issues at hand.

So, before you begin troubleshooting a system, always consider that the need gathering information about a system is the recommended approach to gaining additional insight and familiarity. Look at it this way: the practice of gathering hardware information is not necessarily required, but an investigation of this type may assist you in the search for an eventual diagnosis.

To begin, we will start by running a simple CPU-based hardware report with the following command:

```
# cat /proc/cpuinfo
```

As you will see, the purpose of this command is to output all information related to the CPU model, family, architecture, the cache, and much more. The /proc approach is always a good tradition, but using the following command is generally considered to be a better practice and far easier to use:

```
# lscpu
```

This command will query the system and output all relevant information associated with the CPU in the following manner:

```
Architecture:          x86_64
CPU op-mode(s):        32-bit, 64-bit
Byte Order:            Little Endian
CPU(s):                2
On-line CPU(s) list:   0,1
Thread(s) per core:    1
Core(s) per socket:    2
Socket(s):             1
NUMA node(s):          1
Vendor ID:             GenuineIntel
CPU family:            6
...
```

On the other hand, rather than querying absolutely everything, you can specify criteria by using grep (a subject that we will return to a little later in this chapter) in order to obtain any pertinent information, like this:

```
# lscpu | grep op-mode
```

So, having done this and recorded the results for future reference, we will now continue our investigation by running a simple hardware report with the `lspci` command in the following way:

```
# lspci
```

The result of this command may output something similar to the following information:

```
00:00.0 Host bridge: Intel Corporation 82P965/G965 Memory Controller Hub (rev 02)

00:01.0 PCI bridge: Intel Corporation 82G35 Express PCI Express Root Port (rev 02)

00:05.0 Ethernet controller: Red Hat, Inc Virtio network device

00:0a.0 PCI bridge: Digital Equipment Corporation DECchip 21150

00:0e.0 RAM memory: Red Hat, Inc Virtio memory balloon

00:1d.0 USB controller: Intel Corporation 82801FB/FBM/FR/FW/FRW (ICH6 Family) USB UHCI #1 (rev 02)

00:1d.7 USB controller: Intel Corporation 82801FB/FBM/FR/FW/FRW (ICH6 Family) USB2 EHCI Controller (rev 02)

00:1e.0 PCI bridge: Intel Corporation 82801 PCI Bridge (rev f2)

00:1f.0 ISA bridge: Intel Corporation 82801HB/HR (ICH8/R) LPC Interface Controller (rev 02)
```

The `lspci` command provides all the relevant information concerning the PCI devices of your server, which in turn, can be expanded by employing either the -v option or the alternative -vv / -vvv option(s), depending on the level of detail you require:

```
# lspci -v
# lspci -vv
# lspci -vvv
```

By default, the above commands will provide all the information required by you to confirm whether a device is supported by any of the modules currently installed on your system or not. It is expected that you should only need to do this when hardware upgrades have been implemented, when the system has just been installed, or if you are attempting to familiarize yourself with a new environment. However, in order to simplify this exercise even further, you will be glad to know that a "tree view mode" is also available. The purpose of this facility is to output the associated device ID and show how these values are associated with the relevant bus.

To do this, type the following command:

```
# lspci -t
```

As a troubleshooter, you will be aware that every device must maintain a unique identifier as CentOS, like all other operating systems, will use that identifier to bind a driver to that device. The `lspci` command works by scanning the `/sys` tree for all connected devices, which can also include the connection port, the device type, and class, to name but a few. Having done this, the `lspci` command will then consult `/usr/share/hwdata/pci.ids` to provide the human-readable entries it displays.

For example, you can display the kernel drivers/modules by typing the following `lspci` command with the `-k` option like this:

```
# lspci -k
```

Naturally, during any hardware-based troubleshooting investigation you will want to review the system logs for additional clues, but as we have seen, both the `lscpu` and `lspci` commands are particularly useful when attempting to discover more about the necessary hardware information present on your system.

You can learn more about these commands by reviewing the respective on-board manuals at any time:

```
$ man lscpu
$ man lspci
```

Meanwhile, if you want to practice more, a simple test would be to insert a USB thumb drive and to analyze the findings yourself by paying close attention to the enumeration found within `/var/log/messages`.

 Remember, if you do try this, you are looking at how the system reacted once the USB drive was inserted; you are not necessarily looking at the USB drive itself; the information about which can be obtained with `lsusb`.

On the other hand, in the same way that we can use `grep` with `lscpu`, if you are already feeling comfortable with this type of investigation, then you may like to know that you can also use `grep` with the `lspci` command to discover more about your RAID controller in the following way:

```
# lspci | grep -i raid
```

Now, I am sure you will not be surprised to learn that there are many more commands associated with obtaining hardware information. This includes (but is not limited to) `lsmod, dmidecode hdparm, df -h`, or even `lsblk` and the many others that will be mentioned throughout the course of this book. All of them are useful, but for those who do not want to commit them to memory, a significant amount of information can be found by simply reading the files found within the `/proc` and `/sys` directories like this:

```
# find /proc | less
# find /sys | less
```

Consequently, and before we move on, you should now be aware that when you are dealing with hardware analysis, perfecting your skills is about practice and exposure to a server over the long term. My reason for stating this is based on the notion that a simple installation procedure can serve to identify these problems almost immediately, but without that luxury, and as time goes by, it is possible that the hardware will need replacing or servicing. RAID Battery packs will fail, memory modules will fail, and, on some occasions, it could be that a particular driver has not fully loaded during the most recent reboot. In this situation, you may find that the kernel is flooding the system with random messages to such an extent that it suggests an entirely different issue is causing the problem. So yes, hardware troubleshooting requires a good measure of patience and observation, and it is for this reason that a quick review of both the `lscpu` and `lspci` commands has formed our introduction to troubleshooting CentOS 7.

Understanding dmesg

Before we dive into the subject of log files, I would like to begin by spending a few moments to discuss the importance of the `dmesg` command.

The `dmesg` command is used to record messages from the kernel that are specifically related to the process of hardware detection and configuration. I will not go in too much technical detail at this point, but it is important to realize that these messages are derived from the kernel ring buffer; a condition that can not only prove to be of great assistance because it relates back to the subject of hardware troubleshooting, but one that provides evidence as to why an understanding of the system hardware can reflect in a possible software diagnosis and vice versa.

The `dmesg` file is located in the `/var/log/` directory, but unlike other files that reside in that directory, the basic syntax to view the contents of the `dmesg` file is as follows:

```
# dmesg | less
```

You can page through the results in the usual way, but if you would like to make the timestamp a little easier to read, you may want to invoke the -T option like this:

```
# dmesg -T | less
```

These commands will now provide us with information related to all the hardware drivers loaded into the kernel during the boot sequence. This information will include their status (success or failure), and if a failure is recorded, it will even provide an error message describing why a failure took place. However, as this file can be quite overwhelming, you should use grep to query dmesg in order to streamline this information and simplify the output.

To do this, simply customize the following syntax to suit your needs:

```
# dmesg -T | grep -i memory
```

This command will now display all relevant information regarding the total memory available and shared memory details associated with the server. Of course, similar approaches can be made to read the specific information for USB devices, direct memory access (DMA), or even tty.

For example, you can query dmesg to display hardware information related to any Ethernet ports in the following way:

```
# dmesg -T | grep -i eth0
```

Depending on your system configuration, the output will look similar to this:

```
[Sun Apr 19 04:56:57 2015] IPv6: ADDRCONF(NETDEV_UP): eth0: link is not
ready
```

To extend this approach, you can then modify the previous command in order to discover whether the kernel has detected a specific hard disk. To do this, type:

```
# dmesg -T | grep sda
```

Alternatively, you can then use the -i option to ignore the effects of case sensitivity when searching for tty references:

```
# dmesg | grep -i tty
```

As you will see, the output of the dmesg file is verbose and the information contained within it can be used to troubleshoot almost anything from network cards to storage issues. The demsg file may not give you the answer you are looking for straightaway, but it does provide you with another piece of the puzzle when it is used in combination with the information found in some of the more common log files associated with the CentOS operating system.

Understanding log files

By default, all CentOS system log files can be found in /var/log and a full inventory on your current server can be obtained by typing the following command:

```
# find /var/log
```

With that said, every system is different, and for overall simplicity, you will find that some of the more common log files (associated with a minimal installation of CentOS 7) will include:

- /var/log/messages: This file contains information related to the many native services used by CentOS. This includes (but is not limited to) the kernel logger, the network manager, boot process, mail services, cron jobs, and many other services that do not have their own log files. In many respects, this record can be considered to be a global log file of sorts, and out of habit, it will probably become your first port of call in any troubleshooting process.

- /var/log/boot.log: This file contains information that is reported when the system boots.

- /var/log/maillog: This file contains information that is reported by the default mail server used by the system.

- /var/log/secure: This file contains information that is related to the associated authentication and authorization privileges.

- /var/log/wtmp: This file contains information related to user login records.

- /var/log/btmp: This file contains information related to failed login attempts.

- /var/log/cron: This file contains information related to cron (and anacron).

- /var/log/lastlog: This file contains information related to the binary log that contains all of the last login information.

- /var/log/yum.log: This file contains information related to Yum and reports any activity related to the server's package management tools.

Now, before we continue, I want to draw your attention towards the importance of these files as it is often a good idea to store /var/log in a separate partition to / (root).

A perfect system would maintain a separate partition for /tmp, /usr, and others, but yes, there may be situations where storing your log files on the same partition as / (root) is unavoidable. So remember, if and when the opportunity does arise, you may want to consider storing these directories on a separate filesystem and a separate physical volume (if possible), as this is considered to be good practice with regard to maintaining the overall security, integrity, and performance of the system in question.

However, and having said that, it is also important to recognize that many other packages will create and store logs in other locations. You may even be required to specify these locations yourself, and for this reason, it should be remembered that not all logs are located in /var/log.

For example, if the server in question is hosting one or more websites and storing all the relevant Apache VirtualHost information in a specific /home directory, then the associated log files may be found in a location like this:

```
/path/to/virtualhost/domain1/log/access_log
/path/to/virtualhost/domain1/log/error_log
```

The same can be said of many other packages, and this issue arises because the packages may not have the required privileges to write to that directory, while others are designed to maintain all logging activity within their own installation directory. Therefore, and depending on the nature of your system, you may need to spend a few moments analyzing your server's installation structure in order to locate the appropriate log file(s).

Reading log files and affecting the output

Viewing or reading a log file is very easy and depending on your personal preferences, the basic syntax to view any of these files can be expressed in any of the following formats:

```
# less /var/log/filename
# more /var/log/filename
# cat /var/log/filename
# cat /var/log/filename | less
# cat /var/log/filename | more
```

Remember, depending on the system configuration, you may need root privileges to view a specific log file. The same can be said when you are attempting to make changes to any system files, and for this reason, we will continue as the root user. However, those who use sudo or su (switch user) should change the instructions accordingly.

Log files can vary between applications and services, but the general purpose of these files is to record the time and date of an event and the security level, and to provide a message or general description. Most messages will be general notices or warnings of one type or another, but on certain occasions, errors will also be trapped.

For example, you may see something like this:

```
Dec  4 12:49:05 localhost postfix/postfix-script[1909]: starting the
Postfix mail system
```

Messages like this are quite ordinary and merely explain what is happening and when it happened. Yes, you can safely ignore them, but due to the number of messages you see, some may remark or feel that the system is acting a little oversensitive to the extent that a log file is being flooded with low-level information. This information may serve no real purpose to many, but in some circumstances, you may consider that the information supplied isn't sensitive enough, and more information is needed. In the end, only you can decide what best suits your needs. So, in order to take a case in point, let's increase log sensitivity for the purpose of troubleshooting the system.

To do this, we will begin by running the following command:

```
# cat /proc/sys/kernel/printk
```

The output of the preceding command enables you to view the current settings for the kernel, which, on a typical system, will look like this:

```
4       4       1       7
```

There is a relationship at work here, and it is important that you understand that printk maintains four numeric values that control a number of settings related to the logging of error messages, while every error message in turn maintains its very own log level in order to define the importance of that message.

The log level values can be summarized in the following way:

- 0: Kernel emergency
- 1: Kernel alert; action must be taken immediately
- 2: Condition of the kernel is considered critical
- 3: General kernel, error condition
- 4: General kernel, warning condition
- 5: Kernel notice of a normal but significant condition
- 6: Kernel informational message
- 7: Kernel debug-level messages

So, based on the above information, the log level values of 4, 4, 1, and 7 tell us that the following is now apparent:

- The first value (4) is called the console log level. This numeric value defines the lowest priority of any message printed to the console, thereby implying that the lower the priority, the higher the log level number.

- The second value (4) determines the default log level for all messages that do not maintain an exclusive log level.

- The third value (1) determines the lowest possible log level configuration for the overall console log level. The lower the priority, the higher the log level number.

- The fourth and final value (7) determines the default value for the overall console log level. Again, the lower the priority, the higher the log level number.

Consequently, you are now in a position to consider making changes to the log level through a configuration file found at /etc/sysctl.conf. This file enables you to make fine adjustments to default settings, and it can be accessed with your favorite text editor in the following manner:

```
# nano /etc/sysctl.conf
```

To make the required change use the following syntax:

```
kernel.printk = X X X X
```

Here, the actual value of x is a log level setting taken from the options described earlier.

For example, you can change the number of messages by adding the following line:

```
kernel.printk = 5 4 1 7
```

Of course, such a modification implies a change to the kernel, and for this reason a reboot would be warranted. So, having done this, you will find that the output of running `cat /proc/sys/kernel/printk` should now reflect the new values. However, and as a supplementary note of caution, having considered doing this (and yes, you can easily reverse any changes made), it is important to realize that there are many questions based on the validity of changing these settings. Look at it this way: it may not help you at all, so you should always read around the subject before making these changes in order to confirm that making this alteration will suit your general purposes.

To view the onboard manual, simply use the following command:

```
$ man sysctl
```

On the other hand, for the many other services and applications on your server, you will have additional avenues of investigation to consider and these are generally set by the service or application in question.

A common example of this is Apache. So, if you are debugging a web-based issue related to this service, you may be inclined to open the `httpd` configuration file like this:

```
# nano /etc/httpd/conf/httpd.conf
```

Look or search for the following line:

```
LogLevel warn
```

Then, replace the instruction with a more appropriate setting (before saving the file and restarting the service). In this case, you can use:

```
LogLevel debug
```

Fortunately, it is nice to know that most services and applications do support a form of debugging mode for an improved log output. This will make the log file much more descriptive and easier to work with when troubleshooting the server, but just before we leave this subject, here comes the small print...

When you are working with log files, you should be aware that the information contained within those log files will not always be enough to help you diagnose the issue at hand or discover the cause of a problem. Log files may not only lack the required information, but they can also contain unknown errors and misleading messages. After all, log files only contain a series of (mainly) predefined messages or break points in a package, and these messages have been designed by programmers to make a remark concerning a known event that could have, or has taken place.

> **Remember...**
> When affecting the output of a log file, a verbose and detailed output may raise performance or security issues, while detailed logging can also place an undue burden on the CPU or disk I/O operations.

Based on these circumstances, there are no hard and fast rules because we also know that log files have limitations. So, in the end you will rely on a keen eye for detail and a great deal of patience, and for these reasons alone, you must always learn to "listen to the server" as a whole.

Let's put it this way: the answer is there, but it may not be in the log files. Perseverance and a calm (but firm) hand will win the day, and it is this point of contention that will be echoed throughout the pages of this book.

Using tail to monitor log files

So, armed with the previous information and knowing that log files tend to describe events by specifying the time of occurrence, a level of severity, and a preordained message, the key to success in any troubleshooting scenario is based on an ability to work with these records and manipulate them in such a way that they provide us with the information we require to get the job done.

For the purpose of troubleshooting, one of the most useful commands you will use is known as `tail`. A command-line expression that can be used to read the last lines of a log file is as follows:

```
# tail -n 100 /var/log/maillog
```

Similarly, `tail` can also be used to obtain the most recently added lines like this:

```
# tail -f /var/log/maillog
```

Using this command not only gives you the most recent view of the log file in question, but also ensures that all updates are displayed immediately, which provides an instant way to read log files in a live environment. This approach can be described as the perfect way to troubleshoot Apache, Postfix, Nginx, MySQL, and the many other applications or services your server may be using.

For example, you can view the Apache `access_log` like this:

```
# tail -f /var/log/httpd/access_log
```

To take this feature one step further, let's assume that you wanted to get the last 3,000 lines from a log file knowing that it will not fit within your shell window. To account for this requirement, you can pipe the results with the `less` command like this:

```
# tail -n 3000 /var/log/messages | less
```

In this situation, you can now page the results as required, but having used this technique a few times, I think you would agree that this is far more flexible than using the generic `cat` command; unless of course, you wanted to do something very specific.

Using cat, less, and more

The `cat` command has been with us for a long time and, returning to our previous discussion relating to hardware and the contents of the `/proc` directory, you can use the `cat` command to view detailed information about your server's CPU:

```
# cat /proc/cpuinfo
```

If you wish to know more about the server's memory, you can use:

```
# cat /proc/meminfo
```

Then, there is always the chance to learn more about your devices by typing:

```
# cat /proc/devices
```

As useful as `cat` is, it is also known for providing a dump of the entire content on the screen, a condition that can seem a little unwieldy if the file is greater than 1,000 lines long. So, in these circumstances, the other option is to use the `less` and `more` commands in order to page through specific (static) files in the following way:

```
# less /var/log/messages
# more /var/log/messages
```

However, because more is relatively old, most will argue that less is far superior. The less command is similar to more, but less will allow you to navigate back and forth between paged results. So yes, it's an old joke, but from now on, and wherever possible, always know that less really does mean more.

For example, less allows you to search for a particular string. To do this, simply open the following file using less like this:

```
# less /var/log/messages
```

Now, in the lower left portion of the screen, type /, followed by a string value like this:

```
/error
```

The output will now be adjusted to highlight the search results, and if you are looking for a larger selection of options, simply hit the *H* key while less is open.

Using grep

Now let's consider the need to search the server's log files for specific keywords.

In this situation, you would use the command known as grep, which also becomes a very helpful technique to learn when you would like to perform an advanced string-based search of almost any file on your server.

Let's say you wanted to search for a specific e-mail address in the mail log file. To do this, you would use grep in the following way:

```
# grep "user@domain.tld" /var/log/maillog
```

Taking this one step further, grep can also be used to search in a recursive pattern across one or more files at the same time.

For example, in order to search the log file directory for an IP address (XXX.XXX. XXX.XXX), you would use the grep command in combination with the -R option like this:

```
# grep -R "XXX.XXX.XXX.XXX" /var/log/
```

Similarly, you can add line numbers to the output with the -n option like this:

```
# grep -Rn "XXX.XXX.XXX.XXX" /var/log/
```

Moreover, you will also notice that, during a multi-file based search, the filename is made available for each search result, but by employing the -h option, this can be disabled in the following way:

```
# grep -Rh "XXX.XXX.XXX.XXX" /var/log/
```

You can ignore case with the -i option in the following way:

```
# grep -Ri "XXX.XXX.XXX.XXX" /var/log/
```

Moving beyond this, grep can be used to sort the content of a search result by simply calling the sort command. An alphabetical sort order (a to z) can be achieved by simply adding sort at the end of your original command like this:

```
# grep -R "XXX.XXX.XXX.XXX" /var/log/ | sort
```

A reverse alphabetical sort order (z to a) can be achieved by adding the -r option like this:

```
# grep -R "XXX.XXX.XXX.XXX" /var/log/ | sort -
```

And finally, if you wish to search for more than one value, you can invoke the -E argument like this (but do not include unnecessary white spaces between the pipes):

```
# grep -E "term 1|term 2|term 3" /var/log/messages
```

Of course, grep can do so much more, but for the purpose of troubleshooting, I would now like to draw your attention to one final, but very useful command. Known as diff, this command can be very useful in determining the differences between two files.

Using diff

The diff command is not necessarily considered to be a tool that is associated with log files unless you are comparing backups for a specific purpose. However, the diff command is very useful when comparing changes across an application.

For example, diff will enable you to compare the differences between two Apache configuration files, but by using the -u option, you will be able to include additional information such as the time and date:

```
# diff -u /etc/httpd/conf/httpd.conf /etc/httpd/conf/httpd.conf.backup
```

Now, depending on the size of the files in question and the speed of your server, it may take a few seconds (or even minutes) to complete the task, and yes, I do realize we were digressing from the context of log files, but in time, I think that you will find this command will prove to be very useful.

For example, you may want to compare the contents of two folders using the -rq option to make it recursive like this:

```
# diff -rq /path/to/folder1 /path/to/folder2
```

To learn more about the diff command, simply review the manual by typing:

```
$ man diff
```

Using truncation

So, having been shown how easy it is to work with log files, we should always be mindful that records like this do grow in size, and for this precise reason, they can become difficult to work with as time passes. In fact, you should be aware, oversized log files can impact the system's performance. With this in mind, it is a good idea to monitor any log rotation process and adjust it (on a regular basis) according to need.

Moreover, where log rotation can be critical for a medium- to high-load environment, I would suggest that you manage this solution effectively. However, in situations where the effect of this process proves negligible, the following fail-safe technique will enable you to scrub a log file clean by typing either one of the following commands:

```
# cat /dev/null > /path/to/file
```

Or more appropriately, you can simply use the truncate command like this:

```
# truncate --size 0 /path/to/file
```

This process is known as truncation, and as mentioned, this should remain something of a last resort, as the preceding command will remove all the data contained within the file in question. So remember, if the file contains important information that you may need to review at some time in the future, back it up before you use truncate.

Summary

This chapter was intended to provide an introduction to the subject of troubleshooting CentOS 7 without the intention of burdening you with yet another list of rules, instructions, or procedures that would ill-suit your circumstances or immediate needs. As we know, troubleshooting is a journey, and where the first chapter has served to introduce you to a selection of concepts and methods, every page that follows will ensure that you are one step closer to being at ease with the server you are about to diagnose and repair. So yes, the journey has just begun, and we will now approach the subject of troubleshooting active processes.

References

- The Red Hat customer portal: `https://access.redhat.com/documentation/en-US/Red_Hat_Enterprise_Linux/`

- Syslog Severity Levels: `http://en.wikipedia.org/wiki/Syslog#Severity_levels`

- The Dmesg Wikipedia page: `http://en.wikipedia.org/wiki/Dmesg`

- The Cat Wikipedia page: `http://en.wikipedia.org/wiki/Cat_(Unix)`

- The Grep Wikipedia page: `http://en.wikipedia.org/wiki/Grep`

- The Diff Wikipedia page: `http://en.wikipedia.org/wiki/Diff_utility`

- The Tail Wikipedia page: `http://en.wikipedia.org/wiki/Tail`

- The Less Wikipedia page: `http://en.wikipedia.org/wiki/Less_(Unix)`

2

Troubleshooting Active Processes

A deeper understanding of the underlying active processes in CentOS 7 is an essential skill for any troubleshooter. From high load averages to slow response times, system overloads to dead and dying processes, there comes a time when every server may start to feel sluggish, act impoverished, or fail to respond, and as a consequence, it will require your immediate attention.

In this chapter, we will:

- Learn about memory management, swap, swappiness, and thrashing
- Learn how to analyze active processes using the `vmstat`, `top`, and `ps` commands
- Learn how to monitor the server with `iotop`, `iostat`, and `lsof`
- Learn about system load and `systemd`
- Learn how to find process IDs, identify parent process IDs and orphaned processes, and initiate the various forms of the `kill` signal

Tuning server performance with memory management and swap

Regardless of how you look at it, the question of memory usage remains critical to the life cycle of a system, and whether you are maintaining system health or troubleshooting a particular service or application, you will always need to remember that the use of memory is a critical resource to your system. For this reason, we will begin by calling the `free` command in the following way:

```
# free -m
```

The main elements of the preceding command will look similar to this:

```
            Total     used    free    shared    buffers    cached
Mem:         1837      274    1563         8          0       108
-/+ buffers/cache: 164    1673
Swap:        2063        0    2063
```

In the example shown, I have used the `-m` option to ensure that the output is formatted in megabytes. This makes it easier to read, but for the sake of troubleshooting, rather than trying to understand every numeric value shown, let's reduce the scope of the original output to highlight the relevant area of concern:

```
-/+ buffers/cache: 164    1673
```

The importance of this line is based on the fact that it accounts for the associated buffers and caches to illustrate what memory is currently being used and what is held in reserve. Where the first value indicates how much memory is being used, the second value tells us how much memory is available to our applications. In the example shown, this instance translates into 164 MB of used memory and 1673 MB of available memory.

Bearing this in mind, let me draw your attention to the final line in order that we can examine the importance of swap:

```
Swap:        2063        0    2063
```

Swapping typically occurs when memory usage is impacting performance. As we can see from the preceding example, the first value tells us that there is a total amount of system swap set at 2063 MB, with the second value indicating how much swap is being used (0 MB), while the third value shows the amount of swap that is still available to the system as a whole (2063 MB). So yes, based on the example data shown here, we can conclude that this is a healthy system, and no swap is being used, but while we are here, let's use this time to discover more about the swap space on your system.

To begin, we will revisit the contents of the `proc` directory and reveal the total and used swap size by typing the following command:

```
# cat /proc/swaps
```

Assuming that you understand the output shown, you should then investigate the level of swappiness used by your system with the following command:

```
# cat /proc/sys/vm/swappiness
```

Having done this, you will now see a numeric value between the ranges of 0-100. The numeric value is a percentage and it implies that, if your system has a value of 30, for example, it will begin to use swap memory at 70 percent occupation of RAM.

The default for all Linux systems is usually set with a notional value between 30 to 60, but you can use either of the following commands to temporarily change and modify the swappiness of your system.

This can be achieved by replacing the value of x with a numeric value from 1-100 by typing:

```
# echo X > /proc/sys/vm/swappiness
```

Or more specifically, this can also be achieved with:

```
# sysctl -w vm.swappiness=X
```

If you change your mind at any point, then you have two options in order to ensure that no permanent changes have been made. You can either repeat one of the preceding two commands and return the original values, or issue a full system reboot.

On the other hand, if you want to make the change persist, then you should edit the /etc/sysctl.conf file and add your swappiness preferences in the following way:

```
vm.swappiness=X
```

When complete, simply save and close the file to ensure that the changes take effect.

The level of swappiness controls the tendency of the kernel to move a process out of the physical RAM on to a swap disk. This is memory management at work, but it is important to realize that swapping will not occur immediately, as the level of swappiness is actually expressed as a percentage value. For this reason, the process of swapping should be viewed more as a measurement of preference when using the cache, and as every administrator will know, there is an option for you to clear the swap by using the commands swapoff -a and swapon -a to achieve the desired result.

The golden rule is to realize that a system displaying a level of swappiness close to the maximum value (100) will prefer to begin swapping inactive pages. This is because a value of 100 is a representative of 0 percent occupation of RAM. By comparison, the closer your system is to the lowest value (0), the less likely swapping is to occur as 0 is representative of 100 percent occupation of RAM.

Generally speaking, we would all probably agree that systems with a very large pool of RAM would not benefit from aggressive swapping. However, and just to confuse things further, let's look at it in a different way. We all know that a desktop computer will benefit from a low swappiness value, but in certain situations, you may also find that a system with a large pool of RAM (running batch jobs) may also benefit from a moderate to aggressive swap in a fashion similar to a system that attempts to do a lot but only uses small amounts of RAM. So, in reality, there are no hard and fast rules; the use of swap should be based on the needs of the system in question rather than looking for a single solution that can be applied across the board.

Taking this further, special care and consideration should be taken while making changes to the swapping values as RAM that is not used by an application is used as disk cache. In this situation, by decreasing swappiness, you are actually increasing the chance of that application not being swapped-out, and you are thereby decreasing the overall size of the disk cache. This can make disk access slower. However, if you do increase the preference to swap, then because hard disks are slower than memory modules, it can lead to a slower response time across the overall system. Swapping can be confusing, but by knowing this, we can also appreciate the hidden irony of swappiness. As Newton's third law of motion states, *for every action, there is an equal and opposite reaction*, and finding the optimum swappiness value may require some additional experimentation.

Managing memory with vmstat

A different aspect of memory management can be achieved by using the vmstat command. Considered to be a summary reporting feature associated with memory, processes, and paging, vmstat can be seen in action by typing:

```
# vmstat -a
```

Having used the -a option to call on all active and inactive memory, the most endearing columns shown under vmstat's output are best described as follows:

- si: This column shows the value swapped in from disk
- so: This column shows the value swapped out to disk
- bi: This column shows the value sent to block devices
- bo: This column shows the value received from block devices
- us: This column shows the user time
- sy: This column shows the system time
- id: This column shows the idle time

The display does look quite confusing to begin with, but for our purposes, we want to concentrate on the following columns contained under the swap column:

```
free          si   so
1645452        0    0
```

Where `free` shows the current allocation of free memory, `si` shows page-ins while `so` provides page-outs. Sadly, viewing it by this method alone can be seen to be a little too restrictive for our needs, and so the most effective way to look at this is by managing the output with a delay option being added to the original command like this:

```
# vmstat X N
```

Here, X is a numeric time value expressed in seconds and N indicates the number of times we would like to call `vmstat` itself; a working demonstration of this code format would be as follows:

```
# vmstat 3 5
```

In this example, I have added the values 3 and 5, in which the first number indicates a delay in seconds followed by the second number calling the number of results. In this instance, `vmstat 3 5` will run `vmstat` with a 3-second delay, and it will show a total of 5 updates like this:

```
free          si   so
1645452        0    0
1645452        0    0
1645452        0    0
1645452        0    0
1645452        0    0
```

Alternatively, you can keep `vmstat` running at intervals of N number of seconds by reducing the complexity of the command format to:

```
# vmstat N
```

So, by running `vmstat 10`, `vmstat` will continue to refresh its report of all activity every 10 seconds. However, for more details regarding the time of occurrence, you can use the -t option like this in order to call a similar report with a timestamp:

```
# vmstat -t X N
```

Finally, as the default vmstat command will make a report in kilobytes, to avoid confusion it is often better to ask vmstat to display a report using megabytes with the following expression:

```
# vmstat -S M X N
```

Page-ins (si) are generally expected when you have started an application and the information is "paged-in". However, occasional or intermittent page outs (so) also happen, and this is particularly so during periods when the kernel is freeing up memory. Occurrence of regular page outs (so), or the growth of regular page outs is not wanted. Eventually, should the regularity of these events increase exponentially, then the event will adopt a behavior that is generally referred to as thrashing.

Thrashing is an event that happens when a system is seen to be spending more time managing paging than providing applications or services. It is not necessarily a dire event in itself, but it does indicate that the troubleshooter should re-evaluate the value of particular operations and consider trying to spread them out over different periods of the working day. You can always buy more RAM for your system and this may assist you in the short term, but this will not narrow down the cause, nor will it stop the event from repeating. So, in order to make our lives a little easier, the next step is to use the top command.

Checking the system load with the top command

The top command can be called at any time by typing:

```
# top
```

The top command is the standard command for checking system load (RAM/MEM and CPU). It contains a lot of information related to tasks associated with the kernel; the display is updated in real-time and the highest load factors are expressed as a percentage of CPU or MEM. However, it is important to realize that top may take these values above the expected percentile range. This is because all individual cores are expressed as a percentage and multiple instances of these cores are totaled. For example, a dual core system may have the first core at 70 percent and the second core at 60 percent, and in this instance, top may show a combined result of 130 percent, but you will not know the individual values.

You can use the *M* key to sort `top` by memory, but as you will see, rather than simply showing the amount of free memory (as seen with the `free` command), `top` will provide the swap details you may need in order to make a judgment call against certain operations and tasks. Moreover, you can also extend the functionality of `top` by customizing the output to show a particular user like this:

```
# top -u <username>
```

As you will notice, `top` will automatically refresh; therefore, try to observe it for a few minutes before making any decisions. To assist in this process, you can request that `top` exits after `10` cycles like this:

```
# top -n 10
```

When using `top`, you should always be aware that certain processes are spawned. Known as `child-processes` they will have a tendency to be displayed individually (`httpd` and `php-fpm` are good examples of this), and you can expect that it is these services that will be consuming the most amount of memory.

Having said that, even though a series of child-processes can be seen using a significant amount of RAM, you should avoid the habit of adding the `%MEM` column together as these processes often use shared memory. So, in many respects, you should be aware that the values shown can be misleading, and for this reason, the results provided by `top` should not form the only body of evidence you will want to review before making a final decision.

You can learn more about the top command by reviewing the manual like this:

```
$ man top
```

Monitoring disk I/O with iotop

Every administrator knows that a system can begin to slow down as a result of heavy disk I/O activities. However, in the role of a troubleshooter you will probably want to know which processes or (in the case of multi-user systems) which users are the culprits that and it is for this reason, you will want to turn to `iotop`—a tool that shows a list of the most I/O intensive processes in real time in a top-like interface.

To begin with, you will need to install `iotop` by typing:

```
# yum install iotop
```

The download is only small, and to start a discovery session, simply use the following command:

```
# iotop
```

Running `iotop` without any arguments will result in a list of all existing processes regardless of their disk I/O activities, so if you want `iotop` to only report on processes that are committed to disk I/O activity, you should use the following instead:

```
# iotop -o
```

The output is verbose as it works in a way similar to the `top` command, so familiarity should make you feel at home. However, unlike `top`, `iotop` displays a list of all processes and threads and a measurement of disk activity (total disk read and actual disk read) in order so that you can quickly identify what is impacting any current I/O activity across the server.

You can learn more about `iotop` by reviewing the manual like this:

```
$ man iotop
```

Checking processes with the ps command

For most troubleshooters who want a more complete picture of the processes running on their system, we can employ the `ps` command in the following way:

```
# ps aux | less
```

Alternatively, the information can be displayed in a user-friendly, tree-view mode like this:

```
# ps axjf | less
```

If you prefer a little less detail, try:

```
# ps auxf | less
```

Of course, there are always a lot more options that we can use with `ps`. For example, the command can be piped and applied with `grep` or `tail`, and you can use explicit statements such as `ps -e` (to show every process on the system). Alternatively, you can target a specific process by typing the following command:

```
# ps aux | grep <process_name>
```

Moreover, you can even extend its usage to show every process (except those running as root) with the following variation:

```
# ps -U root -u root -N
```

For a specific user, you can use:

```
# ps -u <username> u
```

Finally, you can then obtain additional security information and output the results to a text file in the following way:

```
# ps axZ > /path/to/filename.txt
```

Based on this, I think you would agree in saying that ps is not only useful but also its flexibility and customization do make it an important tool in the troubleshooter's kitbag. The ps command can be used to display a snapshot of the current processes on the system, but for the purpose of this chapter, our interest lies in the fact that the ps command will also provide us with the relevant process ID. Otherwise referred to in its simpler form as the PID, this essential piece of information will be revisited in just a few moments after we digress a little, to learn a little more about system load.

Checking performance with iostat and lsof

Having already discovered how vmstat can be used to provide statistics related to memory management, when troubleshooting performance-related issues an overburdened CPU is yet another area of concern. For this purpose, we can use the iostat command like this:

```
# iostat
```

However, to display a more interactive CPU utilization report, you can use the -c option (and provide a numeric value measured in seconds, such as 5 seconds) like this:

```
# iostat -c 5
```

Most of the columns should be self-explanatory, but if the system is getting busy, you will see an increase in %iowait, which is used to report on an increase in waiting time for any I/O requests to be completed. Based on this, if the server is transferring or copying a large amount of files, you may also notice additional time being spent at the system level as files will be moved in and out of relevant disk partitions. A feature that is particularly useful when attempting to monitor storage devices in your search for possible bottlenecks is using iostat with a numeric value as follows:

```
# iostat 5
```

As you can see, to check on the read/write operations we have simply added a polling option to iostat. Of course, you can combine this knowledge with the insights gained from running either vmstat -d or vmstat -p <partition_name>, but this command can also be improved with a timestamp by using the -t option like this:

```
# iostat -t 5
```

You should be aware that iostat reports run continuously until the process is cancelled. However, from these observations, it should now make your use of top and all the other commands much more satisfying. The technique of using the following command is particularly welcomed by the fact that you can review a list of open files with the lsof command:

```
# lsof | less
```

 When using lsof, it is important to note that the first column will show you which command is using the file in question, the process ID (PID) of that command, the user, and the name of the file that is open.

So, with that in mind, and realizing how every command discussed in this chapter is connected, let's return to the important subject of system load.

Calculating the system load

The system load is a measure of the amount of processing a computer system is currently performing. It is not the perfect way to measure computer performance, but it does provide the troubleshooter with the additional evidence they need to fix a system.

The expression most commonly associated with calculating load is:

Actual Load = Total Load (uptime) / Number of CPUs

As you probably know the number of CPUs, you can calculate the uptime by reviewing the results of the `top` command or by typing:

```
# uptime
```

The output of the preceding command may look like this:

```
09:59:41 up  2:36,  1 user,  load average: 0.01, 0.02, 0.05
```

The server load is expressed as a value based on 1 minute, 5 minute, and 15 minute read times. So, by looking at the final three values in the preceding output, we can see that, for this system, the average load was `0.01` (at 1 minute), `0.02` (at 5 minutes), and `0.05` (at 15 minutes).

At this current time, the example system shows no sign of fatigue, but as the cause of high-load can vary, this is not to say that the current state of this machine will not alter during the course of a working day. High-load can be the result of database connectivity, disk input and output, poor coding, visitor frequencies for websites, power-hungry applications or e-commerce sites, scripted attacks, spam, batch jobs, and much more. Should you encounter this situation, simply run the `top` command and begin troubleshooting your system in the usual way. In most cases, a short-term solution can be found (especially if your website is receiving a lot of visitors during peak intervals), but only a long-term plan will stop this from happening again.

When troubleshooting load, it is important to know that, when load increases, processors are queued, and if there are multiple processors, the load is evenly distributed across the server's cores to balance the work. The ideal load for a server is generally agreed to be set at a value of 1. This does not mean you should hit the panic button as soon as this value is reached or exceeded, but if you do begin to see double-digit responses for some period of time, then yes, expect that a sluggish server (load value > 1) may now begin to crack under the weight of its workload (load value > 10).

So with this in mind, let's return to the subject of process IDs.

Discovering process IDs with pgrep and systemctl

Rather than using ps, another way of discovering a specific process ID is to use the pgrep command like this:

```
# pgrep <servicename>
```

In most cases, the use of this command will reveal the process ID or PID. However, by using this approach, it is also possible that the output will provide more than one value. So remember, if an application (such as httpd or ssh) provides one or more process IDs, you can safely assume that the lowest number (which represents the first PID generated by the system) is the most important. This value is known as the PPID or parent process ID.

On the other hand, a more succinct method could be based on taking advantage of systemd by using the following command:

```
# systemctl status <service_name>.service
```

The output of the preceding command will look similar to the following sample, and as we can see, the main PID for Apache is 2413:

```
httpd.service - The Apache HTTP Server
    Loaded: loaded (/usr/lib/systemd/system/httpd.service; disabled)
    Active: active (running) since Sun 2014-12-14 01:26:37 GMT; 2min 56s
ago
 Main PID: 2413 (httpd)
    Status: "Total requests: 0; Current requests/sec: 0; Current traffic:
0 B/sec"
    CGroup: /system.slice/httpd.service
            ├─2413 /usr/sbin/httpd -DFOREGROUND
            ├─2414 /usr/sbin/httpd -DFOREGROUND
            ├─2415 /usr/sbin/httpd -DFOREGROUND
            ├─2416 /usr/sbin/httpd -DFOREGROUND
            ├─2417 /usr/sbin/httpd -DFOREGROUND
            └─2418 /usr/sbin/httpd -DFOREGROUND
```

Linux is all about options, and yes, there are many more ways to obtain the required process ID (PID) or parent process ID (PPID), but we will not wade through all the options (both old and new). Based on speed alone, I think you will agree that taking advantage of the systemd command has its own advantages.

More about systemd

The systemd system and service manager is responsible for controlling how services are managed on CentOS 7. Things are very different now, and the consequence of this is to appreciate that, not only have the locations of the scripts changed to /usr/lib/systemd/systemd, but the older commands are to be depreciated to such an extent that (eventually) they will be expunged.

For example, when using systemd to check the status or start or stop a service, you can use one of the following commands:

```
# systemctl status <service_name>.service
# systemctl stop <service_name>.service
# systemctl start <service_name>.service
```

Moreover, rather than using chkconfig, to enable and disable a service during the boot sequence, you should now use:

```
# systemctl enable <service_name>.service
# systemctl disable <service_name>.service
```

You may be in two minds about this approach, but rather than dwelling on the subject of change, let's consider how we can use the new commands to make troubleshooting an active process a little easier. To do this, we shall begin with a simple approach: listing all current services with the following command:

```
# systemctl list-units --type service
```

Everything is now known as a unit, and by realizing this, the same command can be modified to show all mounts as well:

```
# systemctl list-units --type mount
```

Meanwhile, invoking the following command can be used to list all service dependencies:

```
# systemctl list-dependencies <service_name>.service
```

Furthermore, `systemd` also comes with its own version of `top`, and in order to view the processes that are associated with a particular service, you can use the `system-cgtop` command like this:

```
# systemd-cgtop
```

As you will notice, this command provides a summary of all associated processes and indicates the path, number of tasks, percentage of CPU used, memory allocation, and the relative inputs and outputs. It works in a way similar to `top`, but it is different and its use can be modified to output a recursive list of service content as follows:

```
# systemd-cgls
```

The output will look something like this:

```
├─smb.service
│ ├─2472 /usr/sbin/smbd
│ └─2473 /usr/sbin/smbd
├─httpd.service
│ ├─2394 /usr/sbin/httpd -DFOREGROUND
│ ├─2395 /usr/sbin/httpd -DFOREGROUND
│ ├─2396 /usr/sbin/httpd -DFOREGROUND
│ ├─2397 /usr/sbin/httpd -DFOREGROUND
│ ├─2398 /usr/sbin/httpd -DFOREGROUND
│ └─2399 /usr/sbin/httpd -DFOREGROUND
├─polkit.service
│ └─875 /usr/lib/polkit-1/polkitd --no-debug
├─auditd.service
│ └─672 /sbin/auditd -n
```

So, as we can see, in many respects `systemd` is verbose but it does save us time when attempting to retrieve certain information regarding an active process. At this stage, it is important to realize that we have only scratched the surface of `systemd`, but, for the purpose of this chapter, I am sure your continued experience of using it will be both productive and enjoyable.

Issuing the kill signal

The most common reason behind wanting to know a process ID is to pass this information to the `kill` command. The process ID does have other uses, but our primary concern is to remove a problematic service or application by issuing a termination signal (SIGTERM) to the relevant daemon as follows:

```
# kill pid_of_process
```

The `kill` signal instructs the process to terminate, thereby enabling the process in question to perform some basic cleanup operations and exit in an orderly fashion. This approach is known as a "safe kill". However, depending on your situation, a better solution can be to force a service or application to hang up, and thereby enable an automatic reload of the daemon as follows:

```
# kill -1 pid_of_process
```

This command is known as a SIGHUP or `hangover` command. On the other hand, if the process has seemingly crashed, and a safe kill or reload operation fails to make any difference, then by passing the following command, you will be able to literally kill the process in question:

```
# kill -9 pid_of_process
```

The use of option 9 in this command infers a signal kill (SIGKILL), and unlike the original kill order (SIGTERM), this alternative version is issued to the kernel directly, thereby killing the process in a far more abrupt manner. There are no cleanup operations or safe exits with this command, and as a consequence, it is known as a "forced kill".

Finally, to take the issue of a "forced kill" one stage further, it is also quite proper to use the `pkill` command with the following syntax:

```
# pkill -9 httpd
```

Alternatively, you can use the `pgrep` command to ensure that all processes associated with the relevant search term are removed:

```
# pgrep httpd
```

So, having covered the most common usage of the `kill` command, one technique that remains is based on the need to deal with an orphaned process.

Dealing with an orphaned process

Orphaned processes are not common issues, but they do arise, and in order to deal with them, we must begin by matching the displayed PID or PPID with the ID used by the init process itself. Using ps will reveal that both have a PPID equal to 1 and being honest, you will probably realize that there is little difference between an orphaned process and a daemon process with the exception that an orphaned process arises out of error. So, the golden rule here is to remember that an orphaned process can be spotted using a relatively simple technique, and it can be killed in the standard way.

Orphans can arise for a number of reasons and, though they have been adopted by init, you will find that they are still executing commands. For this reason, orphaned processes are potentially dangerous as they continue to starve your system of resources. In some instances, having too many orphans can overload the init process and cause a system hang. This is not common, but the removal of such erroneous daemons is an important task for the troubleshooter, and should your system be prone to such instances, this is something you should keep a constant eye on.

Summary

The purpose of this chapter was to elucidate some concepts with regards to troubleshooting active processes and in this respect we have managed to sweep through the hallways of swap, vmstat, top, ps, process IDs, kill, and pkill. Of course, there are many more utilities at your disposal but for most troubleshooters (beginner and experienced alike), knowing how to monitor and measure memory usage; determining server load; watching for power-greedy applications, services, or users; removing orphaned processes; and using systemd will easily serve you well before we move forward and consider an approach to troubleshoot the network.

References

- The Red Hat Enterprise Linux 7 System Administrators guide: `https://access.redhat.com/documentation/en-US/Red_Hat_Enterprise_Linux/7/html/System_Administrators_Guide/chap-Managing_Services_with_systemd.html`

- The Swappiness Wikipedia page: `http://en.wikipedia.org/wiki/Swappiness`

- The `vmstat` command Wikipedia page: `http://en.wikipedia.org/wiki/Vmstat`

- The `iostat` command Wikipedia page: `http://en.wikipedia.org/wiki/Iostat`

- The `lsof` command Wikipedia page: `http://en.wikipedia.org/wiki/Lsof`

- The `kill` command Wikipedia page: `http://en.wikipedia.org/wiki/Kill_(command)`

- The `pkill` command Wikipedia page: `http://en.wikipedia.org/wiki/Pkill`

- SysVinit to Systemd Cheatsheet: https://fedoraproject.org/wiki/SysVinit_to_Systemd_Cheatsheet

- The Orphans Wikipedia page: http://en.wikipedia.org/wiki/Orphan_process

3
Troubleshooting the Network Environment

From ghost connections to packet errors, stream failures and connectivity errors to missing routes, troubleshooting a network environment can be a slow and arduous process that typically begins with the physical layer. However, once you have confirmed that the physical nodes are working, the next step is to consider and consult the many tools available to your system.

In this chapter, we will:

- Discover the basic tools that will help you troubleshoot a variety of issues related to the network environment. This discussion will include a round-trip tour of `ping`, `dig`, `host`, `traceroute`, and `mtr`.
- Discover how to monitor network connections with the `ss` command.
- Learn how to investigate packet transmissions with `tcpdump`.

Using ping, dig, host, traceroute, and mtr

Some of the most common tools available to a troubleshooter are `ping`, `dig`, `host`, `traceroute`, and `mtr`. Used collectively, these tools provide the troubleshooter with the evidence they need to make a judgment call with respect to almost any network-based issue. This is the basis of the network toolkit, but having said this, it is important to realize that these commands are used for different purposes, and for this reason, we will approach them individually.

The ping command

The ping command is a small utility that can be used to ascertain whether or not a specific IP address can be reached. The ping command is common to most computer systems, and it enables you to query an IP address or a fully qualified domain name in order to check whether there is an available connection.

The basic syntax of the ping command is as follows:

```
# ping <ip_address>
# ping <domain_name>
```

The ping command works by issuing an ICMP echo request to a specified destination in order to verify and check network connectivity, and it is the simplicity of this statement that makes this command such a useful tool when diagnosing any network-based connectivity issue.

For example, if you were to issue a ping request to Google (# ping google.com), then, depending on your networking environment and conditions, the output will look similar to this:

```
PING google.com (216.58.210.14) 56(84) bytes of data.
64 bytes from lhr08s06-in-f14.1e100.net (216.58.210.14): icmp_seq=1 ttl=55 time=10.5 ms
64 bytes from lhr08s06-in-f14.1e100.net (216.58.210.14): icmp_seq=2 ttl=55 time=10.9 ms
64 bytes from lhr08s06-in-f14.1e100.net (216.58.210.14): icmp_seq=3 ttl=55 time=36.2 ms
64 bytes from lhr08s06-in-f14.1e100.net (216.58.210.14): icmp_seq=4 ttl=55 time=11.0 ms
64 bytes from lhr08s06-in-f14.1e100.net (216.58.210.14): icmp_seq=5 ttl=55 time=10.1 ms
64 bytes from lhr08s06-in-f14.1e100.net (216.58.210.14): icmp_seq=6 ttl=55 time=32.0 ms
64 bytes from lhr08s06-in-f14.1e100.net (216.58.210.14): icmp_seq=7 ttl=55 time=10.6 ms
```

These results are an illustration of a successful ping, and it can be described as the journey of an echo request issued by a local computer system to google.com (216.58.210.14).

The request begins on the host computer; it is then sent over the local network and finally across the Internet. Once the request is successfully received, the target will then respond and the time taken to complete this process is measured in order to generate an average response or latency time. However, if there is no response, then it is likely that there is either a physical problem on the network itself, a fundamental issue such as the location is incorrect or non-functional, the target machine not honoring a ping request, or that the host routing table is incorrect.

In online computer games, a ping request (also referred to as a "high ping" or "low ping") is typically associated with the measurement of speed from the local machine to the external game server. For example, a player with a low ping (10 ms for example) will have a better gaming experience than a player with a 180 ms ping.

Moreover, you should also be aware that, if you have a high ping of over 500ms, then it means that any request is taking over half a second to get to the server and back. This condition is noticeable as you will probably be experiencing "frame jitters" or "frame jumps" — a phenomenon known as "rubber banding" in the world of online gameplay.

The `ping` command is simple to use, but in its naked form, it will continue to execute until it is cancelled. In certain situations, this may prove useful, but it is generally easier to invoke the -c option in order to reduce the number of echo requests made and to be provided with a summary of the event.

For example, if you wanted to restrict the number of echo requests made to 4, you need to type the following command:

```
# ping -c 4 google.com
```

In the preceding example, the `ping` command will stop issuing echo requests after 4 cycles, and based on our previous example, the output will look similar to this:

```
PING google.com (216.58.208.78) 56(84) bytes of data.
64 bytes from lhr14s27-in-f14.1e100.net (216.58.208.78): icmp_seq=1
ttl=55 time=11.9 ms
64 bytes from lhr14s27-in-f14.1e100.net (216.58.208.78): icmp_seq=2
ttl=55 time=16.7 ms
64 bytes from lhr14s27-in-f14.1e100.net (216.58.208.78): icmp_seq=3
ttl=55 time=35.4 ms
```

```
64 bytes from lhr14s27-in-f14.1e100.net (216.58.208.78): icmp_seq=4
ttl=55 time=15.1 ms


--- google.com ping statistics ---
4 packets transmitted, 4 received, 0% packet loss, time 3005ms
rtt min/avg/max/mdev = 11.985/19.827/35.462/9.187 ms
```

Now, just before we finish this introduction to the `ping` command, there are a few points regarding any ping requests that should be considered. These points may not necessarily represent a problem, but they will influence the results of a ping test:

- **Distance to the target**: Let's say you live in the U.S., and you try to connect to a server in the EU. In this situation you should expect that the ping would be higher than if you tried to connect to an alternative U.S. server that is closer to you geographically. Further to this, you should expect that there could be speed differences across the various geographical locations.

- **The Internet connection speed**: If you have a low-bandwidth Internet connection (that is, with a poor upload and download speed rating), the ping will take longer to come back to you than if you have a high-bandwidth broadband connection (that is, with a good upload and download speed rating).

- **The hop count**: The hop count is a generic term that refers to the route and servers the ping has to take to reach the destination and back. So, just like it is in the real world, if you live far away from the main train line, you will need to make additional "connections" or "hops" in order to reach the final destination.

The basic principle always states that a low ping is always desirable as it is critical for time-based instructions. However, when conducting a ping test, you must not only consider the total number of pings that actually made it to the target site, but you should also carefully note the average and standard deviation of the pings in question.

Look at it this way: if the pings do not arrive, this may indicate that there could be packet loss due to an unreliable Internet connection between your computer and the destination. However, if the ping rate is low but it shows a widening variable rate over a specific time period, then under certain circumstances, this type of environment is not always preferable when compared to a more constant rate during the same time period.

The dig and host commands

The dig command can be used to verify DNS mappings, Internet connectivity, host addresses, and MX records, and to discover more about any potential reverse DNS issues that can give rise to spam and blacklisting. Made available through the bind-utils package, the information supplied by dig is available in four main parts. This includes a header section (a list of the options used), a question section (the query type), the answer section (the address of the location in question), and the query section (containing statistical information regarding the query time, nameservers, and more). The dig command was introduced to replace nslookup and the basic syntax is as follows:

```
# dig google.com
```

The results will look like this:

```
; <<>> DiG 9.9.4-RedHat-9.9.4-18.el7_1.1 <<>> google.com
;; global options: +cmd
;; Got answer:
;; ->>HEADER<<- opcode: QUERY, status: NOERROR, id: 18657
;; flags: qr rd ra; QUERY: 1, ANSWER: 1, AUTHORITY: 0, ADDITIONAL: 1

;; OPT PSEUDOSECTION:
; EDNS: version: 0, flags:; udp: 512
;; QUESTION SECTION:
;google.com.                    IN      A

;; ANSWER SECTION:
google.com.             299     IN      A       216.58.210.78

;; Query time: 100 msec
;; SERVER: 8.8.8.8#53(8.8.8.8)
;; WHEN: Sat Apr 25 13:45:02 EDT 2015
;; MSG SIZE  rcvd: 55
```

You will notice that there is a lot of information contained within such output, so let's break this down by starting with the global options section:

```
; <<>> DiG 9.9.4-RedHat-9.9.4-18.el7_1.1 <<>> google.com
;; global options: +cmd
```

This is then followed by an output that reports on the answer:

```
;; Got answer:
;; ->>HEADER<<- opcode: QUERY, status: NOERROR, id: 18657
;; flags: qr rd ra; QUERY: 1, ANSWER: 1, AUTHORITY: 0, ADDITIONAL: 1
;; OPT PSEUDOSECTION:
; EDNS: version: 0, flags:; udp: 512
```

Following this, `dig` then repeats the original question:

```
;; QUESTION SECTION:
;google.com.                    IN      A
```

The answer is provided as follows:

```
;; ANSWER SECTION:
google.com.             299     IN      A       216.58.210.78
```

Finally, we are presented with some general statistics about the query itself:

```
;; Query time: 100 msec
;; SERVER: 8.8.8.8#53(8.8.8.8)
;; WHEN: Sat Apr 25 13:45:02 EDT 2015
;; MSG SIZE  rcvd: 55
```

Also, by replacing XXX.XXX.XXX.XXX with a relevant IP address, you can query a specific nameserver like so:

```
# dig google.com @XXX.XXX.XXX.XXX
```

So, if you run the following command:

```
# dig google.com @8.8.8.8
```

You can expect to see the following results:

```
; <<>> DiG 9.9.4-RedHat-9.9.4-18.el7_1.1 <<>> google.com @8.8.8.8
;; global options: +cmd
```

```
;; Got answer:
;; ->>HEADER<<- opcode: QUERY, status: NOERROR, id: 5496
;; flags: qr rd ra; QUERY: 1, ANSWER: 1, AUTHORITY: 0, ADDITIONAL: 1

;; OPT PSEUDOSECTION:
; EDNS: version: 0, flags:; udp: 512
;; QUESTION SECTION:
;google.com.                    IN      A

;; ANSWER SECTION:
google.com.            299     IN      A       216.58.210.78

;; Query time: 92 msec
;; SERVER: 8.8.8.8#53(8.8.8.8)
;; WHEN: Sat Apr 25 13:46:54 EDT 2015
;; MSG SIZE  rcvd: 55
```

Moreover, where the default action of the `dig` command is to search for A records, you can manipulate the `dig` syntax in order to obtain information based on a specific record type as follows:

```
# dig google.com MX
# dig google.com TXT
# dig google.com NS
# dig google.com SOA
```

As an alternative, and in order to generalize the results, you can implement the ANY query in order to obtain as much information as possible by typing:

```
# dig google.com ANY
```

Further to this, the `dig` command can be used to implement a reverse lookup in order to obtain relevant DNS information based on a specific IP address.

This can be achieved by typing:

```
# dig -x 8.8.8.8
```

The preceding command will subsequently respond with an answer in the following way:

```
; <<>> DiG 9.9.4-RedHat-9.9.4-18.el7_1.1 <<>> -x 8.8.8.8
;; global options: +cmd
;; Got answer:
;; ->>HEADER<<- opcode: QUERY, status: NOERROR, id: 34651
;; flags: qr rd ra; QUERY: 1, ANSWER: 1, AUTHORITY: 0, ADDITIONAL: 1

;; OPT PSEUDOSECTION:
; EDNS: version: 0, flags:; udp: 512
;; QUESTION SECTION:
;8.8.8.8.in-addr.arpa.          IN      PTR

;; ANSWER SECTION:
8.8.8.8.in-addr.arpa.    21599   IN      PTR     google-public-dns-a.
google.com.

;; Query time: 35 msec
;; SERVER: 8.8.8.8#53(8.8.8.8)
;; WHEN: Sat Apr 25 13:49:13 EDT 2015
;; MSG SIZE  rcvd: 93
```

So, as you can see, `dig` is a flexible command-line tool that will enable you to perform a valid DNS query. Its output is verbose, but it can be encapsulated with the `+short` switch to provide a reduced and concise answer like so:

```
# dig -x 209.132.183.81 +short
```

The above command should respond in the following way:

```
www.redhat.com.
```

The `dig` command is an incredibly useful tool for troubleshooting a network, and its success is primarily associated with its ability to return the question, answer, authority, and additional sections.

However, and having said that, the alternative is to use the `host` command in the following way:

```
# host -a google.com
```

The `host` command works in a similar way to the `dig` command but its output looks like this:

```
Trying "google.com"
;; ->>HEADER<<- opcode: QUERY, status: NOERROR, id: 60735
;; flags: qr rd ra; QUERY: 1, ANSWER: 14, AUTHORITY: 0, ADDITIONAL: 0

;; QUESTION SECTION:
;google.com.                    IN      ANY

;; ANSWER SECTION:
google.com.             299     IN      A       216.58.210.78
google.com.             299     IN      AAAA    2a00:1450:4009:801::200e
google.com.             21599   IN      NS      ns3.google.com.
google.com.             21599   IN      TYPE257 \# 19
0005697373756573796D616E7465632E636F6D
google.com.             599     IN      MX      20 alt1.aspmx.1.google.
com.
google.com.             21599   IN      NS      ns4.google.com.
google.com.             21599   IN      SOA     ns1.google.com. dns-
admin.google.com. 2015041501 7200 1800 1209600 300
google.com.             3599    IN      TXT     "v=spf1 include:_spf.
google.com ip4:216.73.93.70/31 ip4:216.73.93.72/31 ~all"
google.com.             599     IN      MX      40 alt3.aspmx.1.google.
com.
google.com.             21599   IN      NS      ns1.google.com.
google.com.             599     IN      MX      30 alt2.aspmx.1.google.
com.
google.com.             599     IN      MX      50 alt4.aspmx.1.google.
com.
google.com.             21599   IN      NS      ns2.google.com.
google.com.             599     IN      MX      10 aspmx.1.google.com.
```

As you can see, the `host` command serves a similar purpose to `dig` and yet it is far more succinct.

For example, a basic `host` query will be as follows:

```
# host www.google.com
```

The returned output will look like this:

```
www.google.com has address 216.58.210.68
www.google.com has IPv6 address 2a00:1450:4009:801::2004
```

Alternatively, you can specify a third-party DNS server in the following way:

```
# host www.redhat.com 8.8.8.8
```

The output of this will report on the use of an alternative DNS server and look like this:

```
Using domain server:
Name: 8.8.8.8
Address: 8.8.8.8#53
Aliases:


www.redhat.com is an alias for wildcard.redhat.com.edgekey.net.
wildcard.redhat.com.edgekey.net is an alias for wildcard.redhat.com.
edgekey.net.globalredir.akadns.net.
wildcard.redhat.com.edgekey.net.globalredir.akadns.net is an alias for
e1890.b.akamaiedge.net.
e1890.b.akamaiedge.net has address 23.195.127.72
```

Finally, host can perform reverse lookups like this:

```
# host XXX.XXX.XXX.XXX
```

So, let's say you run a reverse lookup against Red Hat's Akamai Edge server with the following command:

```
# host 23.195.127.72
```

The output will look like this:

```
72.127.195.23.in-addr.arpa domain name pointer a23-195-127-72.deploy.
static.akamaitechnologies.com.
```

So look at it this way: for the purpose of troubleshooting a network, you can use either dig or host. Both of the commands are similar in terms of what they can be used for and what they can achieve, but where host offers simplicity, dig serves to provide a more advanced and script-worthy option.

The traceroute command

The `traceroute` command is designed to show the pathway to a remote destination and the delays that occur at every stop. Most administrators are familiar with `traceroute` and it maintains three primary objectives that can be summarized as follows:

- To provide details of the entire path that a packet will traverse
- To provide the names and the identity of the devices and routers found on that path
- To report on network latency as a result of assessing the time taken to send and receive data to each device on a given path

In simple terms, the `traceroute` command is a tool that verifies the path your data will take without using any data, and the syntax used is based on the following:

```
# traceroute google.com
```

The output will provide the specified host, the IP address for that domain, the maximum number of hops required, and the size of the packet that will be used. The subsequent lines then report the hop number, hostname, IP address, and packet round-trip times. Of course, you can also avoid reverse DNS with the use of the `-n` option in the following way:

```
# traceroute -n google.com
```

The `traceroute` command sends three packets with each TTL and will display the round-trip time (RTT), which indicates the time difference between the issuing of a probe and the receipt of a response packet. This is useful in discovering network bottlenecks, and if you begin to see asterisks (*), then this suggests that there is a potential problem routing to that host as the asterisks can indicate packet loss or a dropped packet. However, it is also important to realize that interpreting `traceroute` can rely on an understanding and appreciation of its inherent quirks.

The `traceroute` command is recognized to be the cornerstone of TCP/IP troubleshooting. It begins by issuing a UDP-based packet with a TTL value of 1. If the packet reaches the target, then the gateway sends a response packet and reports its findings. However, if the packet does not reach the target, then the recipient gateway will decrease the TTL by the value of 1. If the TTL value reaches 0, then the gateway will drop the packet and report the results after a new packet is issued with an increased value in order to circumvent the same gateway in the next phase. This process is repeated until the target host is reached or the maximum TTL value is reached.

There are three different types of `traceroute` implementation that cover UDP, TCP, and ICMP.

For example, if you wanted to use the ICMP variation, you will type:

```
# traceroute -I google.com
```

Again, you can bypass DNS with the -n option like this:

```
# traceroute -I -n 8.8.8.8
```

This variation will work in a manner similar to the previous examples that use UDP in which the `traceroute` program will send echo requests, and the hops in between will reply. However, unlike the UDP version, the process will use ICMP.

The final way is to use a TCP variation in the following way:

```
# traceroute -T google.com
```

In many respects, the TCP option is probably the most effective method, as most networks will allow for this traffic. This is particularly so if you are targeting port 80. However, there are no hard and fast rules to determine which version of `traceroute` you can or want to use. The rules will be set by the network configuration, as some networks will block UDP requests by default (typically, ports 33434 to 33534). So, based on this, why not try them all and see what provides the best results for your environment.

Let's look at it this way: knowing how `traceroute` works is winning only half the battle. If `traceroute` can reach the host, but not the target, then it is likely that the issue is with the target. However, if `traceroute` cannot reach the host, then it is likely that the issue lies with the route itself, which not only consists of some routers denying `traceroute` packets, but others that show remarkable differences in bandwidth and latency, firewalls, and a whole host of other traps that are filtering `traceroute` packets. In this situation, multiple targets should be selected (you should also consider sending your requests using UDP, ICMP, and TCP to circumvent any network issues), and given that the Internet is asymmetric by nature, it is generally a good idea to perform a `traceroute` action in both directions in order to judge the overall network efficiency.

On the whole, `traceroute` is an excellent tool, but it can be misleading, so be cautious in analyzing the results and always supplement your work with additional investigation.

The mtr command

As an alternative to `traceroute`, there is the `mtr` command. On some Linux systems, you will need to run this as the root user or in conjunction with `sudo`, but whatever method you use, the syntax of this command is very simple and it works in the following way:

```
# mtr google.com
```

The output may look similar to `traceroute`, but the display is in real-time, thereby enabling you to monitor trends and averages to reflect how network performance changes over time. So unlike `traceroute`, instead of merely taking a snapshot of a single journey, by using `mtr` you are able to check for intermittent packet issues by gathering data over a longer period of time. Moreover, as an alternative to real-time updates, `mtr` will also provide a reporting option that will issue the results of 10 packets to each hop encountered:

```
# mtr --report google.com
```

So, upon reflection, it can be argued that `mtr` is superior to `traceroute` at monitoring network connectivity. It certainly has many advantages and it can provide a significant amount of detail, but knowing that you cannot control how the world will work outside your internal network, the seasoned troubleshooter should always remain vigilant and choose to examine every tool at his disposal.

Monitoring network connections with the ss command

The socket statistics command (`ss`) is the successor to `netstat`; it is not only faster, but it is also able to display more information. However, unlike `netstat`, which obtains its information from the various files contained within the `/proc` directory, the `ss` command obtains its information directly from the kernel space.

The basic syntax of the `ss` command is as follows:

```
# ss | less
```

Using this syntax, we have simply called for an output of all TCP, UDP, and Unix socket connections with an optional pipe to less in order to ensure that the results can be seen on screen. Of course, this command can be combined with either the -t, -u or, -x option to restrict any output to show either TCP, UDP, or Unix socket connections respectively, but in order to make the output more informative, you will probably want to combine one of these additional options with the -a option in order to report on both connected and listening sockets like this:

```
# ss -ta
```

As you will notice, in the preceding instance we are only reporting on the current TCP environment and it can be changed to suit UDP (ss -ua) or Unix socket connections (ss -xa) in a similar way. However, if you enjoy a degree of precision, you will be comforted to know that the ss command can be combined with a query by using the -A option like this:

```
# ss -a -A tcp
```

Restricting the output does serve to make the information far more concise, but to take this one stage further, additional filters can be applied using the following syntax:

```
# ss [ OPTIONS ] [ STATE-FILTER ] [ ADDRESS-FILTER ]
```

For example, where all standard TCP states are accounted for, you can display all established IPv4 TCP sockets in the following way:

```
# ss -t4 state established
```

You can show all closed TCP states like this:

```
# ss -t4 state closed
```

Now, it can be argued that using the ss command will perform in a similar way to using netstat -a. This in part is true, but (and remember that you can replace -t with -u or -x) given the ability to increase the speed of execution by not resolving hostnames (ss -nt), show only listening sockets (ss -ltn), show socket memory usage (ss -t -m), show processes using particular sockets (ss -t -p), print the process name (ss -ltp), display either IPv4 or IPv6 (ss -tl4 or ss -tl6), and show time information (ss -tn -o), you will notice that we have merely scratched the surface of the ss command.

For example, you can even run a query to discover who was using port 22 (SSH) by using the following syntax:

```
# ss -lpn | grep 22
```

Alternatively, you can use the following syntax to show all ports connected from a remote IP address:

```
# ss dst XXX.XXX.XXX.XXX
```

Then filter the query to a specific port with the following variation:

```
# ss dst XXX.XXX.XXX.XXX:22
```

Remember, familiarity with your networking environment will always help, and armed with this command, you should be in a better position to recognize problematic connections before they take hold.

Packet analysis with tcpdump

The `tcpdump` command is a packet analyzer that is able to capture and provide a description of the traffic being transmitted across a network interface. It is common to most flavors of Linux, and it provides access to a unique view of the network at the packet level that can prove vital when troubleshooting the network environment.

The basic syntax for using `tcpdump` is expressed in the following way:

```
# tcpdump -i <device_name>
```

You can also specify a protocol like this:

```
# tcpdump -i <device_name> tcp
```

While a port value can be used in the following way:

```
# tcpdump -i <device_name> port 22
```

Verbosity options can be issued by using -v or -vv, while DNS can be avoided with the -n option. However, because `tcpdump` will continue running until the request is cancelled, it is always preferable to use the -c option in order to capture a pre-determined number of events in the following way:

```
# tcpdump -c 10 -i <device_name>
```

Taking this one step further, you can capture 10 packets from a specific IP address by calling either the src option (source) or the dst option (destination) like this:

```
# tcpdump -c 10 -i <device_name> src XXX.XXX.XXX.XXX
```

While the device name itself can be obtained by running the following option:

```
# tcpdump -D
```

The tcpdump command can be run in both the read and write modes. However, where the latter implies the use of the -w option that will cause tcpdump to save the packet data to a file for later analysis, the former, signified by the use of the -r option, will determine that tcpdump will read from a saved packet file only. As you will come to realize, when in the write mode you should specify the relevant device name (that is eth0), but in both cases, only packets that match an expression will be matched and displayed.

For example, in read mode, the basic syntax of this commands looks like this:

```
# tcpdump -r <file_name>
```

While in write mode, you can send the entire Ethernet frame for further analysis in the following way:

```
# tcpdump -w /path/to/file -i <device_name>
```

So as you can see, the most common application of tcpdump is to verify whether the process of two-way communication is working. The tcpdump command can be used to record network segments, and while recognizing this fact, we have merely scratched the surface of its flexibility.

For this reason, I hope you can already see how this small utility can become an important tool when troubleshooting your networking environment.

Summary

The purpose of this chapter was to provide a starting point when attempting to troubleshoot areas of concern across the network environment. Of course, there is always more to learn, and knowing this will take you on a journey that goes far beyond the basic syntax of dig, ping, or even tcpdump. However, having toured a number of commands and utilities, you can now see how becoming an effective troubleshooter is quickly becoming an obtainable goal. To further our cause, we will now set our sights on the need to troubleshoot package management.

References

- The TCP Wikipedia page: `http://en.wikipedia.org/wiki/Transmission_Control_Protocol`
- The Ping Wikipedia page: `http://en.wikipedia.org/wiki/Ping_(networking_utility)`
- The Traceroute Wikipedia page: `http://en.wikipedia.org/wiki/Traceroute`
- The `ss` command official page: `http://www.cyberciti.biz/files/ss.html`
- The ARP Wikipedia page: `http://en.wikipedia.org/wiki/Address_Resolution_Protocol`
- The `dig` command Wikipedia page: `http://en.wikipedia.org/wiki/Dig_(command)`
- The `tcpdump` Wikipedia page: `http://en.wikipedia.org/wiki/Tcpdump`

4
Troubleshooting Package Management and System Upgrades

The Yellowdog Updater, Modified (Yum) has been with us for a while. It is easy to use and it serves to reduce the complexity of dependency management when installing or upgrading CentOS packages. More commonly referred to as Yum, this chapter will be assuming that you are already proficient in its fundamental usage (including installing packages, updating packages, removing packages, and searching for packages) as our intention is to continue the overall premise of this book by approaching the subject of package management and system upgrades.

In this chapter, we will:

- Learn how to gather software information with RPM and YUM
- Learn how to use Yum plugins to make the process of troubleshooting an easier task
- Troubleshoot issues relating to package installation and updates
- Discover how to extend the system and install additional Yum repositories
- Learn how to download an RPM package with Yum
- Learn how to restore an RPM database
- Discuss the complexities of managing minor system upgrades

Gathering software information

Before starting to tackle YUM, we will deviate a little by turning our attention towards the process of gathering the necessary software information in order to discover more about the system in general.

To do this, we will begin by running the following command:

```
# cat /etc/redhat-release; lscpu | grep -i arch; yum repolist all; ls
-alsh /etc/yum.repos.d;
```

At this stage, I will not explain every command shown in the above example, but you will notice that the output is verbose, and it does a good job of detailing the CentOS release information. The information displayed includes details regarding the overall architecture of the server; the domain, time, and date information, and finally, the extent, status, and permissions of the repository list used by Yum.

So far so good, but what if I need to know about the RPM-based packages that are installed on the server? Rather than wading through an entire series of configuration files (or even making an educated guess), why not simply use the following command:

```
# rpm -qa | sort | less
```

As you can see, depending on what is installed on your server, the above command will output an extensive (or on the other hand, a relatively small) list of RPM-based packages. If this is too detailed, and you merely want a quick idea as to what the installation history could be, you can simply display the total number of RPM-based packages by typing the following command:

```
# rpm -qa | wc -l
```

As we have used the wc command, the output will be restricted to a numeric value representing the information requested. It may be too simplistic or vague for your exact needs, but it will give you a firm grounding with regard to the current usage of the server in question (especially if this task is repeated over specific time periods).

So, why stop there? If you feel rather more inquisitive, then you can also request information regarding which Yum packages are installed by typing the following command:

```
# yum list installed | sort | less
```

At this stage, you may be asking, what is the difference between `yum list installed` and the previously mentioned `rpm -qa` command? In simple terms, the former Yum-based command will also list the package dependencies, so you should expect to see far more detail in the output.

Again, this listing can either be extensive or not depending on the purpose of the server in question, but for those of you who enjoy the benefits of good housekeeping, this function can be improved by printing the output to a file of your choice like this:

```
# yum list installed | sort > /path/to/filename.txt
```

Again, nothing too complicated at this stage, but before we round off these initial steps, it is important to realize that we have just exposed some of the secrets of a previously unknown CentOS server. Our familiarity with the system is now growing, and as a consequence of our activity, you will now feel far more comfortable and at ease with your new surroundings. After all, when a server goes down and everyone else is panicking, the confidence gained here will count towards your eventual success.

Using Yum plugins

Yum is one of the most widely used package management tools, but many administrators are unaware that it comes complete with a plugin system that can be used to extend its capabilities. It would be true to say that many of these plugins are installed by default, but as it is assumed you know nothing about the current system (which may often be the case for any troubleshooter), we will begin by installing the `yum-skip-broken` set of packages.

So, let' s start by typing the following command:

```
# yum install yum-skip-broken
```

Having done this (and confirmed that this set of packages is now available to the system), we can now use the `--skip-broken` plugin to approach any situation in which you want to update or upgrade a certain package, which is refused due to a report of broken dependencies.

To do this, a combination of the following commands can be used:

```
# yum update --skip-broken && yum upgrade --skip-broken
```

Of course, you can simplify the above command to suit your own purpose (by breaking it over two separate lines), but it should be noted that the reason an error occurs in these circumstances is often related to the mistake of mixing (incompatible) third-party repositories. In this respect, and in order to achieve a long-term solution, you will need to reduce the number of third-party repositories used. However, before attempting this, you should review the past transactions of Yum in order to ascertain how this will affect the system.

This can be achieved by typing the following command:

```
# yum history
```

The above command will now generate a list of all the past operations undertaken by Yum, thereby affording a level of detail that can prove to be quite useful when attempting to debug a broken service, correct a package dependency, or assist in the process of reducing the number (or reliance) on third-party repositories. Moreover, from the list this command generates, you will also notice that each transaction carries a unique identifier.

The unique identifier can be used to obtain even more information about a particular event by typing:

```
# yum history info <unique_identifier>
```

Alternatively, in situations where this level of detail is not required, you can always obtain a summary of all recent events by typing the following command:

```
# yum history summary
```

That being said, and while we are on the subject of Yum plugins, you should also be aware that changelog information is not directly available from the Yum package manager. Again, this type of information can be useful, but in order to follow this line of enquiry, you will need to install the changelog plugin by typing the following command:

```
# yum install yum-plugin-changelog
```

Having done this, you will then be able to query the Yum changelog like this:

```
# yum changelog all <package_name>
```

As this output can be quite overwhelming, it is helpful to know that you do have the ability to restrict the information displayed by simply replacing the term all with a numeric value that indicates the number of records to show. So, in the case of wanting to read the 5 most recent updates to Postfix, you would type:

```
# yum changelog 5 postfix
```

Moreover, with this plugin installed, you can review the relevant `changelog` information prior to any package installation by typing the following command:

```
# yum update --changelog
```

This is a small but interesting feature that can be extended to show all recent `changelog` information by typing:

```
# yum changelog all recent
```

Or, you can view all obsolete packages by typing:

```
# yum changelog all obsoletes
```

Finally, and before we close our discussion on using Yum plugins, there may be a situation that calls on the need to utilize `yum-utils`, and if it is not currently available to the system in question, you can install it by typing:

```
# yum install yum-utils
```

This addition makes package management a breeze when you consider the whole host of issues that can include the removal of orphaned or duplicate packages and the resolution of package cleanup operations.

For example, to remove orphaned packages, you can type:

```
# package-cleanup --orphans
```

To remove duplicates, you can use:

```
# package-cleanup --dupes
```

To facilitate the removal of old kernels, you can type:

```
# package-cleanup --oldkernels
```

With reference to the above example, if your system maintains a number of old kernels you can query them by running the command, `rpm -q kernel`. As you will see, this simple operation can provide the information you need in order to decide to whether the option to free disk space is available or not. If old kernels can be seen, you can remove them in the usual way. However, rather than suggesting that you need to do this, in uncovering this feature, my intention was to prove that `yum-utils` has many interesting features that should be explored, as it is an underrated aspect of Yum that can play an essential role when troubleshooting package management.

Fixing Yum operations

Now, it is important to realize that in many instances, the general cause of an error with Yum can begin with the network environment, an issue related to disk space, mixed repositories, or even the DNS settings on the system. However, there are occasions when a few common procedural errors will need rectifying by flushing Yum itself with one or more of the following range of commands.

To purge old package information, you should use:

```
# yum clean headers
```

To clean all cached packages, use the following command:

```
# yum clean packages
```

To clean all cached XML-based data, use this:

```
# yum clean metadata
```

However, if you would like to flush the Yum cache in its entirety (including all headers, metadata, download packages, and more), you can always use the following command to complete the process:

```
# yum clean all
```

Installing additional Yum repositories

Installing additional repositories is not necessarily considered to be a troubleshooter's task, but it does serve to alleviate many issues regarding package dependencies and attempts to keep your system relevant within a Dev/Ops environment.

In the following text, I have included instructions for some of the most popular repositories. However, you should realize that the locations of these repositories will be different for alternative versions of CentOS, and that these links will be updated over time. Additional information can be found at the end of this chapter for future reference.

EPEL

The **Extra Packages for Enterprise Linux** (EPEL) repository provides useful software packages that are not included in the official CentOS Linux repositories, some of which will be covered in the following chapters of this book. It is also a requirement for many other third-party repositories.

For CentOS 7, you should follow this procedure to install the EPEL repository:

```
# cd /root
# wget https://dl.fedoraproject.org/pub/epel/7/x86_64/e/epel-release-7-5.
noarch.rpm
# yum install epel-release-7-5.noarch.rpm
```

Having completed the relevant steps, simply confirm that you would like to continue with the installation and then type the following command to ensure it is enabled:

```
# yum repolist all
```

EPEL is generally considered to be a base repository that is often required by many other repositories, and given the desire to keep our system current, I have included the procedures to install both the Remi and IUS repositories. However, with a heavy note of caution, I would suggest using only one of them to avoid any possible conflicts that may arise from employing them both on the same system.

Remi

The Remi repository depends on the EPEL repository and provides newer versions of the software to the core CentOS Linux repositories; so having installed this repository, you may expect to see several updates to the CentOS system the next time you run yum update.

For CentOS 7, you should follow this procedure to install the Remi repository:

```
# cd /root
# wget http://rpms.famillecollet.com/enterprise/remi-release-7.rpm
# rpm -Uvh remi-release-7*.rpm
```

By default, the Remi repository is disabled; to enable it, we will need to update the configuration file and mark it as active.

To do this, open the following file in your favorite text editor like this:

```
# nano /etc/yum.repos.d/remi.repo
```

Now, change:

```
    enabled = 0
```

To read:

```
    enabled = 1
```

Moreover, if you want to use the PHP 5.5 libraries, simply uncomment the `[remi-php55]` reference in the same file `remi.repo`. When done, save and close the file before typing the following command to ensure it is enabled:

```
# yum repolist all
```

The IUS repository

As an alternative to Remi, the IUS repository also provides newer versions of software to the core CentOS Linux repositories, but the developers stress that IUS tends to use different package names in order to avoid conflicts that can arise from software version updates. This simple approach to package names has gained a lot of traction within the CentOS community as a whole as this level of control can be very useful within a mission critical environment. The IUS repository depends on the EPEL repository, but again, I would advise against mixing this repository with other sources.

For CentOS 7, you should follow this procedure to install the IUS repository:

```
# cd /root
# wget http://dl.iuscommunity.org/pub/ius/stable/CentOS/7/x86_64/ius-release-1.0-13.ius.centos7.noarch.rpm
# rpm -Uvh ius-release*.rpm
```

Moreover, given that the IUS repository works in a unique way, you should be aware that there is a package called `yum-plugin-replace` that is used to assist in the process of upgrading from stock packages to IUS `packageXY` style packages.

Again, I have provided a link to additional materials at the end of this chapter on how this tool can be used (and it is expected that these instructions may change over time), but at this present time, you can begin by typing:

```
# yum install yum-plugin-replace
```

Overall, regardless of whether you use Remi or IUS, remember, the golden rule is not to mix them, but regardless of which of these repository you choose, it is expected that either of them will serve you well.

Downloading an RPM package with Yum

If there is ever an occasion where you need to download a package but not install it, then this can be achieved with Yum. However, to begin this process, you need to ensure that your system maintains the following utility:

```
# yum install yum-plugin-downloadonly
```

In most cases, it may already be installed (as it forms part of the `yum-utils` package mentioned previously), but having completed this task (or confirmed that it is already present), you can simply download the required package to a directory of your choice by customizing the following command:

```
# yum install <package_name> --downloadonly --downloaddir=/path/to/folder
```

For example, and to make sense of the the preceding command, you can download Samba and all of its dependencies to a user-based directory by typing:

```
# yum install samba --downloadonly --downloaddir=/home/username
```

Alternatively, you can also invoke the following variation, although this version of the command will assume that the download will be stored in your current location:

```
# yumdownloader <package_name>
```

Having done this, the next step will be to extract the contents of the package downloaded using `yumdownloader` in order to access the relevant RPM using the following command:

```
# rpm2cpio <package_name> | cpio -idmv
```

The `cpio` command is typically used for backups, and its function is to facilitate the transport of files in and out of a `cpio` archive. It works in a way similar to `tar`, but unlike `tar`, `cpio` can work in conjunction with the `find` command.

For example, to make a back up, you can begin by accessing the relevant directory like this:

```
# cd /path/to/directory
```

List the directory contents to ensure that everything is present:

```
# ls -altr
```

Now, run the command for backing up the directory in the following way:

```
# find . -print | cpio -ocv > /path/to/backup-name.cpio
```

So, in a few short steps, we have discovered how to download a package through Yum and to extract the relevant package data using the `cpio` command, a process that may prove to be most useful when troubleshooting a particular service or application that requires a dependency. This may or may not be the first time you have seen the `cpio` command, and yes, you won't be surprised to know that we have only scratched the surface of how it can be used. So, with that in mind, I would encourage you to learn more about it, as you will find that it will prove to be very useful at some point in the future.

Additional information about the `cpio` command can be found at the end of this chapter, but for reference, you can begin your journey by typing:

```
$ man cpio
```

Diagnosing a corrupt RPM database

RPM is a package management tool that stores information about software packages in its own database located at `/var/lib/rpm`, but on some occasions, it has been observed that this database can fail. If such an event does take place, then this can render the use of the `rpm` command useless, and in this situation, it is not uncommon to find that the system will begin exhibiting signs of trouble related to any Yum- or RPM-based processes.

For example, during a typical Yum update procedure, you could witness the following message:

```
"error: cannot open Packages database in /var/lib/rpm"
```

At this point, I cannot help but stress the importance of a good backup strategy, but as a troubleshooter, this may be out of your control. Therefore, in such circumstances, the rudimentary process of restoring the RPM database can be diagnosed by completing the following steps:

```
# cd /var/lib/rpm
# rm -rf __db*
# rpm -v --rebuilddb
```

Having completed the above steps, you should be able to run various sanity checks in order to confirm that there are no segmentation errors by using one or more of the following commands:

```
# db_verify Packages
# db_stat -CA
# rpm -qa
# rpm -Va
# yum update
```

For example, having run the command `db_verify Packages`, you should see the following type of output:

```
BDB5105 Verification of Packages succeeded.
```

Hopefully, this procedure will fix the issue. However, it is important to realize that this process is not definitive and it can fail. Look at it this way, in order to avoid this situation, a regular backup of `/var/lib/rpm` should be considered to be common practice on all CentOS/RHEL-based systems, and if verification of packages process fails, you will need to consider a full restore from a recent backup.

Minor release upgrades

For CentOS 7 users, the ease of completing a minor release upgrade is simply a matter of using Yum but, as always, you should perform a full backup before proceeding.

The precise nature of the types of files you should back up will differ from system to system, but it will include configuration files, important system files, user data, databases, web versioning, and application files. Moreover, if you are using proprietary software, you should confirm the feasibility of any upgrades with the original developers prior to completing an update.

So, having taken all these measures into account, when possible, I would recommend the process of backing up the entire system, and in this respect, you can be rest assured that you will have a copy of everything.

To begin the process of a minor upgrade, you can view the current CentOS release information by typing:

```
# cat /etc/redhat-release
```

You can then view the Linux information with:

```
# uname -mrs
```

Now, before you invoke Yum to obtain a list of updated packages, it is always a good idea to begin by typing:

```
# yum clean all
```

Then, follow the instruction to purge Yum, as follows:

```
# yum check-update
```

You will now be presented with a list of updates for the system in question. These pending updates will be displayed in a familiar format, and they will detail the package name and versioning.

If you wish to update the system, use the following command:

```
# yum update
```

The time required by any update can vary, so you may need to be patient. However, having successfully completed this step, you may want to consider rebooting the system. The practice of rebooting a system is particularly advantageous if the updates need to effect any changes to the kernel during the boot phase.

To do this, type:

```
# reboot
```

Finally, after the reboot is complete, you can verify your system updates using:

```
# uname -a
```

Now, run one or more of the following commands to ensure that all services and applications are running correctly:

```
# tail -f /var/log/messages
# netstat -tulpn
# ps aux | less
```

Summary

In this chapter, we have taken a whirlwind tour through the intricacies of troubleshooting package management. There is always much more ground to cover, but for the purpose of system administration, you have not only discovered a series of tools that can be used to overcome a wealth of common issues related to Yum, but we have also discussed the ability to extend Yum through a variety of plugins, install third-party repositories, enable Yum to download RPM packages, and restore an RPM database.

So, as you can see, and before we move on to a discussion regarding users, directories, and files, with some lateral thinking and a little practice, you should now be well on your way to being able to troubleshoot an entire host of problems and make almost any package management issue a thing of the past.

References

- The CentOS upgrade tool: http://wiki.centos.org/TipsAndTricks/CentOSUpgradeTool

- How do I upgrade from Enterprise Linux 6 to Red Hat Enterprise Linux 7?: https://access.redhat.com/solutions/637583

- The cpio Wikipedia page: http://en.wikipedia.org/wiki/Cpio

- The `cpio` command: `http://www.gnu.org/software/cpio/manual/cpio.html`
- EPEL/epel7beta-faq: `https://fedoraproject.org/wiki/EPEL/epel7beta-faq`
- EPEL/epel7: `https://fedoraproject.org/wiki/EPEL/epel7`
- Index of /pub/epel/7/x86_64/e: `http://dl.fedoraproject.org/pub/epel/7/x86_64/e/`
- Les RPM de Remi - Blog: `http://blog.famillecollet.com/pages/Config-en`
- Index of Remi: `http://rpms.famillecollet.com/enterprise/`
- IUS Community Project: `https://iuscommunity.org/pages/IUSClientUsageGuide.html`
- Index of /pub/ius/stable/CentOS: `http://dl.iuscommunity.org/pub/ius/stable/CentOS/`
- The IUS package replacement guide: `https://iuscommunity.org/pages/IUSClientUsageGuide.html`
- The ATrpms repository: `http://atrpms.net/about/`
- The Nux repository: `http://li.nux.ro/repos.html`
- The RPM home page: `http://rpm.org`
- The RPM recovery diagnostics: `http://www.rpm.org/wiki/Docs/RpmRecovery`

5
Troubleshooting Users, Directories, and Files

Unlike the previous subjects discussed so far, the process of troubleshooting users, directories, and files can be seen as a continual process that requires constant attention during the life time of the server. It will become an every day event, and for this reason, we will start with the basic principles of user management with the intention to show you how to restore the default file and folder permissions, recover lost files, and take you on a journey through many more associated themes in order to prepare you for a variety of issues that any professional troubleshooter may encounter.

In this chapter, we will:

- Learn how to effectively manage the process of adding, deleting, modifying users, and implementing system-wide changes with `login.defs`
- Discover how to monitor user activity with `utmpdump`
- Learn how to reset the root password and initiate root-based logging to achieve improved command-line security audits
- Learn how to recover lost data with Scalpel
- Learn how to restore default permissions and ownership
- Discover more about the XFS filesystem by discovering how to run ongoing repairs and investigate defragmentation
- Learn how to audit directories and files
- Discover how to visualize directories and files

Users

User management is a fundamental skill associated with the need to manage a server, and in this respect, it will inevitably represent a milestone when troubleshooting any system. So, with this in mind, we will quickly analyze the process of managing users in order to dispel any confusion.

Adding users and forcing a password change

You can add a new user (and create a home folder for them) by using the following command:

```
# adduser <username>
```

You can provide the new user with a password like this:

```
# passwd <username>
```

Alternatively, if you would like to force a password reset, thereby implying that a user must reset his/her password, then the following command will suffice:

```
# chage -d 0 <username>
```

In addition, you can null a password for a specific user by typing:

```
# usermod -p "" <username>
```

However, if you would like to grant this new user the ability to use sudo, then type:

```
# gpasswd -a <username> wheel
```

Finally, if you would like to know more about a user, using the following command, will disclose their current properties:

```
# id <username>
```

Deleting users

The action of deleting a user account is generally straightforward, but it can involve a number of stages that can be forgotten. Therefore, to avoid any future issues across extensive systems with a large amount of users, prior to deleting a user from the system, the account should be locked in the following way:

```
# passwd -l <username>
```

You will then want to back up the home directory using `tar` before confirming if there are any active processes attributed to this account by typing:

```
# ps aux | grep -i <username>
```

Having done this, you can now proceed to kill any active processes attributed to that account by using the following command:

```
# pkill -u <username>
```

Or, you can remove individual process IDs like this:

```
# kill -9 <pid>
```

By using `pkill`, you are invoking the SIGTERM command, which will streamline the task of removing any active process associated with that account. So, at this stage, you should now consider removing any files, print jobs, and re-assign or delete any `cron` jobs associated with that account.

You can do this by typing the following command:

```
# find / -user <username> -print
```

Having done this, you can safely delete a user with:

```
# userdel -r <username>
```

Using the `-r` option will also remove the home directory associated with that account, but if you would like to delete the user, their home directory, and remove any SELinux mappings, you should use:

```
# userdel -rZ <username>
```

However, if you encounter any difficulties, then you can always use the force option in the following way:

```
# userdel -rfZ <username>
```

Finally, you will need to consider removing any SSH keys associated with that user. Ensure that `sudo` or `su` is not enabled for that account, and then proceed to work through your applications and services one at a time (including database, e-mail, file sharing, htaccess, web directories, CGI files, and more) while reassigning new settings to any common accounts that the system may use.

Modifying a user

One of the most useful aspects of user management for a troubleshooter is being able to modify an existing user account. There could be many reasons as to why this task is required, but the best illustration of this skill would begin with changing the default `adduser` attributes in the following file:

```
# nano /etc/default/useradd
```

From here, you can redefine what shell is used, the default location of the home directories, and whether a default mail spool is set.

For example, you can use this technique to change the default location of the home directories from /home to /home/<companyname>. However, if you prefer to do this manually (on a case-by-case basis), in order to change the location of the home directory, you need to use the `usermod` command in conjunction with the -d option (the path to the new directory) and the -m option (to move the contents of the current home directory), like this:

```
# usermod -m -d /path/to/new/home/directory <username>
```

When running the preceding command, it is important to realize that a PID will be displayed on the console if the user is currently using the system and this must be killed before any modifications can be made.

Finally, should the need arise to transfer an existing user to a different group, then this can be achieved by invoking the -g option like so:

```
# usermod -g <new_group_name> <username>
```

However, having done this, and just as you would for deleting a user, you must manually change the ownership of any `crontab` files or jobs and complete the process by making any relevant changes to any remaining (related/existing) services as well.

Meet login.defs

When it comes to managing users, an alternative or long-term approach is to consider altering the default settings found in /etc/login.defs so that you can alter the behavior of the delete command.

For example, consider you find the following line commented out like this:

```
#USERDEL_CMD        /usr/sbin/userdel_local
```

Uncomment this line and it will ensure that all `at/cron/print` jobs are removed. Moreover, you can also use the `login.defs` file to determine the default values assigned to the user mail directory, password encryption method, password expiry period, `userid`, `groupid`, and many more.

Monitoring user activity with utmpdump

Keeping track of user activity is one of the most essential skills associated with any Linux administrator. In situations where user management may be the cause of a troubleshooting session, we can make use of `utmpdump`.

User histories are typically stored in the following locations:

- `/var/run/utmp`: The purpose of this binary is to record open sessions. You can review the contents of this file with `utmpdump /var/run/utmp`.

- `/var/run/wtmp`: The purpose of this binary is to record connection histories. You can review the contents of this file with `utmpdump /var/log/wtmp`.

- `/var/log/btmp`. The purpose of this binary is to record failed login attempts. You can review the contents of this file with `utmpdump /var/log/btmp`.

Taking this one step further, you can also review the current history of logged sessions contained within `/var/run/wtmp` by typing:

```
# last
```

You can review the current history of logged sessions contained within `/var/run/btmp` by typing:

```
# lastb
```

However, as a simple review of these files is slightly redundant for our needs, you can read the current status of these files with the following commands:

```
# stat /var/run/utmp
# stat /var/log/wtmp
# stat /var/log/btmp
```

The output of these commands may look similar to this:

```
Access: 2015-04-26 07:29:13.143818061 -0400
Modify: 2015-04-26 06:24:02.444728081 -0400
Change: 2015-04-26 06:24:02.444728081 -0400
```

Now, given that binary files cannot be viewed using basic reading commands such as cat, less, and more, rather than simply relying on basic commands such as last, who, lastb, and others, a different approach is to use the utmpdump command like this:

```
# utmpdump /path/to/binary
```

So, as we have already mentioned earlier, in the case of wanting to read /var/run/utmp, you can use the following command:

```
# utmpdump /var/run/utmp
```

While the remaining files would be accessible with:

```
# utmpdump /var/log/wtmp
# utmpdump /var/log/btmp
```

So, having used all three commands, you will then notice that the output is in a familiar format with the most obvious difference being that the results of wtmp are displayed in reverse order as opposed to both utmp and btmp which are displayed in chronological order.

The results of utmpdump are formatted in the following way:

- The first column displays a session identifier; the value 7 is typically associated with a new login event, while the value 8 is associated with a logout event.
- The second column displays a PID.
- The third column can hold a relative variable based on either of the following:
    - ~~, indicating a run-level or system reboot change
    - bw, or a bootwait process
    - A numeric or TTY value
    - A character/digit that indicates a PTY value (the pseudo terminal).
- The fourth column can sometimes remain empty or maintain an associated username, runlevel, or reboot value.
- The fifth column (if this information is available), will display the TTY or PTY value.
- The sixth column will display the identity of the remote host. In most local cases, you will only see a runlevel message at most, but for remote access, you will see an IP address or name.

- The seventh column will display the remote host's IP address, or it will show 0.0.0.0 for local access.

- The eighth, and final column, will indicate the time and date information as to when the record was created.

You should also be aware that columns six and seven will show identical information if no DNS resolution is performed.

So, with the preceding information in mind, with a bit of practice, and using the skills we discovered in the previous chapters, utmpdump can be used to perform a wide range of queries such as displaying general access information like this:

```
# utmpdump /var/log/wtmp
```

Further to this, you can use grep to show the details of specific records.

For example, if you wanted to display the records of a particular user from wtmp, you will type:

```
# utmpdump /var/log/wtmp | grep <username>
```

Taking this one step further, you can use grep to identify the number of logins from a particular IP address in the following way:

```
# utmpdump /var/log/wtmp | grep XXX.XXX.XXX.XXX
```

Or use the following syntax to check how many times root accessed the system:

```
# utmpdump /var/log/wtmp | grep root
```

Then use the following command to monitor the number of failed login attempts:

```
# utmpdump /var/log/btmp
```

Remember, the output of btmp should be minimal, given that this binary will show a variety of issues related to the use of incorrect passwords being used or attempts to log in with an unknown username. The latter of which is particularly important when a tty1 was shown to be used, as this will indicate that an unknown person had access to a terminal on your machine. Look at it this way, noticing such an important issue may inspire you to run a security audit on access privileges and keys by creating a basic text-based output file with the following command:

```
# utmpdump /var/log/btmp > btmp-YYYY-MM-DD.txt
```

Resetting the root password and enhancing logging

With the release of CentOS 7, you may find that the process of resetting the root password has changed. So, in the event that you forget the root password, you will need to follow these important steps.

Boot the computer and press the *E* key during the kernel screen phase. On the next screen, scroll down the text and look for the following line:

```
root=/dev/mapper/centos-root ro
```

Now, replace the letters `ro` with the following:

```
rw init=/sysroot/bin/sh
```

It should then look like this:

```
root=/dev/mapper/centos-root rw init=/sysroot/bin/sh
```

When done, press *Control* + *X* or *Ctrl* + *X* to boot into the single user mode using the bash shell `/sysroot/bin/sh`.

In the single user mode, type:

chroot /sysroot

After the hash sign (#), type:

passwd root

Follow the onscreen instructions and proceed to reset the password, but if you do need to update `SELINUX` use the command `touch /.autorelabel` before you do anything else.

When you are ready to finish, type the following command to access the machine in the usual way:

exit

Now, reboot your system in the usual way:

reboot

Well done! You should now be able to gain full access to the system using the new root password. However, if you decide to update the logging for all system commands, simply open the following file in your favorite text editor like this:

nano /etc/bashrc

Scroll down to the bottom and add the following line:

```
readonly PROMPT_COMMAND='history -a >(logger -t "$USER[$PWD] $SSH_
CONNECTION")'
```

Having done this, you will now find that all the SSH-based command-line activity is logged through /var/log/messages like this:

```
Jan 11 11:38:14 centurion1 journal: root[/root] 192.168.1.17 53421
192.168.1.183 22: last

Jan 11 11:38:26 centurion1 journal: root[/var/log] 192.168.1.17 53421
192.168.1.183 22: cd /var/log

Jan 11 11:38:32 centurion1 journal: root[/var/log] 192.168.1.17 53421
192.168.1.183 22: cat messages

Jan 11 11:38:49 centurion1 journal: root[/var/log] 192.168.1.17 53421
192.168.1.183 22: last
```

Recovering lost or deleted files with Scalpel

If a file has been accidentally deleted from the system, you can use a small utility called Scalpel to recover it. Scalpel is a faster alternative to Foremost, which was originally developed by the United States Air Force Office of Special Investigations and The Center for Information Systems Security Studies and Research. Today, it is a tool that is generally associated with both digital forensics investigation and file recovery, and you can install it by typing the following command:

```
# yum install scalpel
```

You will need the EPEL repository to complete this process (which is discussed in a previous chapter), but when you are ready, simply update the following configuration file to determine what types of files you would like to search for:

```
# nano /etc/scalpel.conf
```

Having done this, you should now create a recovery directory, and then you should move to the /etc directory in order to use scalpel.conf like this:

```
# cd /etc
```

You can run a scan on a relevant device by customizing the following command:

```
# scalpel /path/to/device -o /path/to/recovery/directory
```

An example of the preceding command would look like this:

```
# scalpel /dev/sda1 -o /tmp/recovery-session1
```

Scalpel will begin by creating work queues, but be mindful that the entire operation will take some time to complete. In simple terms, the actual time taken to complete a scan will depend on the disk size, the number of deleted files, the power of the machine in general, and other activities that the system is currently performing.

You can view the findings by using the `ls` command like this:

```
# ls -la /path/to/recovery/directory
```

Finally, and before you get started, you should be aware that a new recovery directory must be created every time you run Scalpel (so you may want to consider using an alternative hard disk) as the results will be maintained by a single audit file.

This particular file can be viewed by typing:

```
# less /path/to/recovery/directory/audit.txt
```

Remember, Scalpel will work with a variety of filesystem formats or raw partitions, and in this respect, it can be seen as a very useful tool for any troubleshooter.

You can learn more about Scalpel by reviewing the manual like this:

```
# man scalpel
```

Restoring file and directory permissions

File and directory permissions are important, and to view the current state of all the files in a particular directory, you can run the following command:

```
# ll
```

Alternatively, you can target a particular directory by running:

```
# ll /path/to/directory
```

However, in a situation where someone has mistakenly changed the permissions of a particular system-based file or folder this calamitous situation can be rectified with the following RPM-based commands:

```
# rpm --setugids PACKAGENAME
```

```
# rpm --setperms PACKAGENAME
```

On the other hand, should it be the case that an entire directory has been mistakenly updated with `chown` or the `chmod` commands, the following commands will prove more useful:

```
# for package in $(rpm -qa); do rpm --setugids $package; done
# for package in $(rpm -qa); do rpm --setperms $package; done
```

Based on the commands shown preceding, the first command will serve to reset all the file and folder ownerships values to the default state, while the second command will serve to reset the relative file permissions. So having run these commands, it is possible that you will see the following messages:

```
chgrp: cannot access '/usr/share/man/zh_TW/man5x': No such file or
directory
chown: cannot access '/usr/share/man/zh_TW/man6': No such file or
directory
chgrp: cannot access '/usr/share/man/zh_TW/man6': No such file or
directory
chown: cannot access '/usr/share/man/zh_TW/man6x': No such file or
directory
```

Don't worry! Regardless of which file or directory is listed, such notices can be safely ignored.

Working with and extending the XFS filesystem

Originally developed at Silicon Graphics in 1993, the main purpose of XFS is to not only support the creation of large filesystems that will allow for metadata journaling, but to provide a technology that can be defragmented and enlarged while mounted and active. This information may or may not be of much use to you as a troubleshooter, but you should be aware that the default filesystem now employed by the most recent release of CentOS is known as XFS. If you did not customize the partitions to any great extent, then you may find that XFS is the filesystem you will be dealing with.

You can quickly confirm the structure of your system with the following command:

```
# df -Th
```

The preceding command (the disk size and partitions ignored) can result in something similar to the following output:

```
Filesystem              Type      Size  Used Avail Use% Mounted on
/dev/mapper/centos-root xfs        42G  1.5G   40G   4% /
devtmpfs                devtmpfs  913M     0  913M   0% /dev
tmpfs                   tmpfs     919M     0  919M   0% /dev/shm
tmpfs                   tmpfs     919M  8.4M  911M   1% /run
tmpfs                   tmpfs     919M     0  919M   0% /sys/fs/cgroup
/dev/sda1               xfs       494M  139M  356M  29% /boot
/dev/mapper/centos-home xfs        21G   33M   21G   1% /home
```

The wording `xfs` under the column labeled `type` is what we are looking for. If it is found that your server does use the XFS filesystem, then the XFS tools and utilities file `xfsprogs.x86_64` can be installed with the following command:

```
# yum install xfsprogs
```

Generally speaking, you should be aware that XFS can prove to be the source of a subtle loss of performance if the server system is relatively small. In these circumstances ext4 tends to be faster with some single threaded and metadata intensive workloads. Moreover, as shrinking support is not available to XFS, you should know that this technology does not allow the filesystem to be reduced in size even when un-mounted. For this reason, you may want to stay with ext4 when big filesystems or big files are not required.

Looking at the bigger picture, you will be comforted to know that the basic syntax required to create an XFS is similar to other filesystems:

```
# mkfs.xfs /dev/device
```

So, no surprises there, and due to the similarities with other filesystems, I will assume that you are comfortable completing the rest of this procedure. However, before you begin, you should always be aware of the server's hardware configuration before starting this operation, as there may be a few notable issues you may want to be aware of before concluding this operation.

For example, let's say the server exceeded 2 TB. So having completed the initial `fdisk` operations to build the filesystem layout, (prior to mounting) you may decide to benchmark the system because every good troubleshooter knows that XFS enables write barriers to ensure filesystem integrity.

You can achieve this simple operation by typing:

```
# mount -o inode64 /dev/device /mount/point
```

By default, write barriers will serve to preserve the filesystem from issues relating to power failure, resets, and system crashes, but if your hardware maintains a good write cache, then it may seem more prudent to disable the write barrier in order to reduce the impact on performance.

In this respect, you can mount the device in the following way:

```
# mount -o nobarrier /dev/device /mount/point
```

On completion, you can always request further information about a specific volume with the following syntax:

```
# xfs_info /mount/point
```

So as we can see, XFS does come with a lot of good features and tools, but when it comes to the process of troubleshooting a server, it is precisely these differences that could be the cause of the problem.

In this respect, and as we will now see, XFS should be treated in a different way to a comparable ext3- or ext4-based system. However, if you need to extend the filesystem, then you will be happy to know that XFS comes complete with a standard tool known as `xfs_growfs` that can be used in the following way:

```
# xfs_growfs -d /mount/point
```

Assuming that you have reviewed the man pages, it would be obvious to state that your syntax would use the `-d` option in order to grow the filesystem to the maximum size supported by the device.

Running repairs on XFS

XFS was created with the intention to support extremely large filesystems. It performs incredibly well under a heavy load and scales with large files, but as a result, it is also susceptible to damage, and it is with this in mind that we now consider a set of tools that will enable us to troubleshoot the server and restore the filesystem.

Known as `xfs_repair`, this tool is used to confirm filesystem consistency and repair any problems that are found. This process will not restore lost data, but it should restore the filesystem on the device in question.

The basic syntax used by `xfs_repair` is as follows:

```
# xfs_repair /mount/point
```

However, to avoid any error messages, the procedure will then require that you should initially umount the device in question. In this respect, the entire procedure will be as follows:

```
# umount /mount/point
# xfs_repair /mount/point
```

The resulting output will then proceed to run through a series of phases and confirm the relevant events. Once complete, simply remount the device in the usual way to complete the task. However, on the chance that xfs_repair fails, repeat this process again but do your research on the respective error messages.

If xfs_repair fails to fix the consistency problems on a third occasion, depending on the error messages, you may want to consider an alternative rescue plan for the server, as it should be assumed that data recovery can only be made from backups.

Having said that, it is possible that you can consider additional steps to recover the device in question.

At this current stage, you should assume that data recovery can only be made from backups and your plan is now based on the recovery of the filesystem only. However, having said this, it is important to remember that you should not take any action that will impact the production environment.

It may be possible to restore files from the disk by backing up and restoring the files on the filesystem. To do this, mount the filesystem in the read-only mode and proceed to make a backup with xfsdump. From this point onwards, you will want to remake the partition and restore the files with xfsrestore. Check man xfsdump and man xfsrestore for further details.

Alternatively, if log recovery is unsuccessful, it may be possible to recover some of the data by mounting the filesystem in the read-only mode with the no recover option. This will avoid running the log recovery process but, by using this method, the filesystem is unlikely to be consistent, and it is to be expected that not all of the data will be returned.

The xfs_repair utility is designed to repair filesystems. It is size independent (treating both large and small filesystems equally), but unlike other repair tools, it will not run at boot and it will only initiate logging at mount in order to ensure a consistent filesystem. In cases where xfs_repair encounters a damaged log file, it will not be able to repair the filesystem, so in the event that this does happen, you will need to clear the relevant log, mount and then un-mount the XFS filesystem, which is done by adding the -L option to force log zeroing like this:

```
# xfs_repair -L /mount/point
```

Remember, resetting the log can leave the filesystem in an inconsistent state. This can, and generally does, result in the loss of data and/or data corruption. So, only apply these methods with the intention to restore the filesystem alone. Remember, the `xfs_repair` command is not intended to restore the data on that filesystem.

Investigating fragmentation on XFS

In situations where the filesystem is acting sluggishly, it is possible that fragmentation is impacting your server. In this instance, and if you suspect that fragmentation has occurred or is occurring, then simply run the following command on the relevant device:

```
# xfs_db -c frag -r /mount/point
```

By using this command, we are causing `xfs_db` to open the filesystem in a read-only mode (`-r` option) and passing a command (`-c` option) to get the file fragmentation data (`frag`) for the device in question. When we use the `frag` command, it will only return information relevant to the file data in the filesystem as opposed to concerning itself with the fragmentation of free space. So, depending on the specific nature of your system, the resulting output could look similar to this:

```
fragmentation factor 0.31%
```

In a more severe case, it could report the following output:

```
fragmentation factor 93.39%
```

By drawing your attention to the fragmentation factor (expressed as a percentage) in the preceding examples, you may have found at least one reason as to why your server requires troubleshooting. Fixing this situation would be a matter of calling the filesystem organizer utility, otherwise known as `xfs_fsr`. We would simply require the system to reorganize our partition or device to optimize disk usage in a similar way to a Microsoft Windows desktop. In this respect, the most basic syntax for using `xfs_fsr` would be as follows:

```
# xfs_fsr /path/to/device
```

Whereas, for a single file, you can use:

```
# xfs_fsr /path/to/file
```

However, given that the period of time for these events to complete can be quite long, a more succinct use of this command would be to specify a list of filesystems to reorganize (-m), a time option -t calculated in seconds, and the verbose option -v for a clear indication of what is happening, as follows:

```
# xfs_fsr -m /etc/mtab -t 7200 -v
```

The corresponding output will then display the number of extents that are both before and after the inode. By default, xfs_fsr will make ten passes before completing the process unless you decide to reduce the number of passes by using the option -p like this:

```
# xfs_fsr -m /etc/mtab -t 7200 -v -p 2
```

You should be aware that xfs_fsr should not be used to defragment the whole system as this is generally regarded to be unnecessary as it can give rise to free space fragmentation, so you can complete this task in stages in the knowledge that the operation can be interrupted cleanly. This will leave the filesystem in a consistent state. If you interrupt the process (using *Ctrl* + *C*), xfs_fsr will save the defragmentation process to the following location:

```
# /var/tmp/.fsrlast_xfs
```

However, before you dive in, the real issue here is that this fragmentation issue should be approached with caution on a live system, as proceeding to defragment a device or partition during periods of high-load will place an unnecessary burden on your server. So in this instance, the best course of action is to run xfs_fsr at a time when the relevant device or partition is not at full load or during lighter working periods.

Finally, and having completed the process of defragmentation, you can confirm the extent of the work performed with the following command:

```
# xfs_db -c frag -r /mount/point
```

So having completed these simple actions, or necessitated a future (and possibly repeat) cron job, you should now notice an immediate improvement with regard to the speed at which files and folders can be moved and transferred.

Auditing directories and files

An important task related to troubleshooting can arise from an understanding of activities commonly associated with the action of reading and writing files. CentOS 7 provides a simple utility for this. Known as `auditd`, this service (or daemon) starts during the boot process. Events are recorded to an associated log file found at `/var/log/audit` and as it runs in the background, you can check the current service status with:

```
# systemctl status | grep audit
```

It is possible to customize the auditing service and you can have direct access to manage the log file size, location, and associated attributes by accessing the following file with your favorite text editor:

```
# nano /etc/audit/auditd.conf
```

Moreover, if you do not wish to lose any auditing data, you are able to disable the machine when an audit cannot be performed. To do this, open the configuration file `auditd.conf` and add or modify the following lines:

```
max_log_file_action = keep_logs
space_left_action = email
action_mail_acct = root
admin_space_left_action = halt
```

This action is severe and it is not something to jump into without doing your homework, but it will serve to remove the default action of rotating log files and replace it with an instruction to e-mail the root user.

Finally, should you wish to take advantage of the audit service flag for every process, simply open `/etc/default/grub` and add the following argument to the kernel line:

```
audit=1
```

Remember to regenerate grub with the following command and reboot:

```
# grub2-mkconfig -o /boot/grub2/grub.cfg
```

This will ensure that an auditable flag is set for every process after the boot sequence has been initiated and, for even greater simplicity, we can then consider building a unique set of rules by editing the following file:

```
# nano /etc/audit/rules.d/audit.rules
```

To make this as easy as possible, the best approach is to find your server's `stig.rules` file at `/usr/share/doc/audit-X.X.X/stig.rules` and copy it to `/etc/audit/rules.d/audit.rules`. Based on the current package version (in my case), the `stig.rules` file can be found at `/usr/share/doc/audit-2.3.3/stig.rules`. Consequently, I ran the following command to create a default rule set:

```
# cp /usr/share/doc/audit-2.3.3/stig.rules /etc/audit/rules.d/audit.rules
```

So, having customized the rules and restarted the `auditd` service, you will discover that a query can be initiated with the following syntax:

```
# ausearch -f /path/to/directory/or/file
# ausearch -f /path/to/directory/or/file | less
# ausearch -f /path/to/directory/or/file -i | less
```

As an alternative to this, you can use `aureport` to produce a series of audits in the following way:

To monitor unusual behavior, you can use:

```
# aureport --key --summary
```

To build a report on user logins, you can use:

```
# aureport -l -i -ts yesterday -te today
```

To review access violations, you can try:

```
# ausearch --key access --raw | aureport --file --summary
```

Finally, to review anomalies, you can use:

```
# aureport --anomaly
```

Of course, we haven't covered every aspect of the auditing service, but the preceding examples should get you started. Remember, all of the examples shown can be added to a cron job and, should you wish to know more, the `aureport` manual can always be viewed any time by typing:

```
# man ausearch
# man aureport
```

Visualizing directories and files

Good administration starts with good housekeeping, and for this reason, the maintenance of detailed records regarding your server's layout is generally considered to be a good starting point for any Linux administrator. Such a task not only allows you to keep abreast of any changes made to the system as a whole, but it can be a useful approach to debugging. Moreover, because you may have inherited this system, or shared access with a number of administrators, it is probably a good idea to consider running an up-to-date inventory of the changes made.

All directories, folders, and files accessible to a specific Linux-based system are arranged in a single tree. Starting from root (/), this hierarchy may consist of either local or remote files, local or remote filesystem(s), and local or remote block devices.

To view this tree, simply ensure that you have installed the following package:

```
# yum install tree
```

By default, the tree command will begin indexing from your current location, so to begin, simply change your location to the boot directory like this:

```
# cd /boot
```

Now, run the following command:

```
# tree
```

The tree command is technically described as *a recursive directory listing command* that displays the content of your server in a tree-like format. It is highly customizable, so if you prefer to target a specific directory from your current location, you can use:

```
# tree /path/to/folder
```

You may have noticed that the tree command does not show hidden files by default. Therefore, in order to see all files (including all hidden files), use the -a option like this:

```
# tree -a /path/to/folder
```

However, if you would like the tree function to restrict itself to displaying folder names only, you should use the -d option like this:

```
# tree -d /path/to/folder
```

If it all looks a little plain and ordinary, you can add some color to the output with the -C option like this:

```
# tree -C /path/to/folder
```

Finally, you can combine the preceding options to print the output to a text file by typing:

```
# tree > /folder/name/filename.txt
```

For example, if you wanted to maintain a list of files in one or more directories showing the current permissions, you can use the -p option like this:

```
# tree -p > /folder/name/filename.txt
```

Alternatively, if you would prefer to display the output with embedded HTML code for export, try:

```
# tree -H /path/to/folder
```

So, regardless of whether you have adopted a new server, or you are troubled by the number of users accessing and writing files to that server, the tree function provides a relative solution to keeping a visual audit of your server, or your devices, by typing:

```
# tree -d /sys/devices
```

So why not combine this with a cron job? Then you can regularly keep an eye on the rise of any potential problems or even maintain a visual record of when those changes took place. In this respect you could assert that the tree package is a very useful tool, and to learn more you can review the manual at any time by typing:

```
# man tree
```

Summary

In this chapter, we have approached a number of topics related to users, directories, and files, while introducing some related themes associated with the release of the XFS filesystem. From forcing password changes to visualizing the directory structure, restoring the root password to understanding the need for disk defragmentation, our pursuit of troubleshooting CentOS 7 has gone some way to show that the knowledge gained from resolving fundamental system-based issues directly relate to the ongoing human-based issues. It would be true to say that you can never rehearse a disastrous scenario because every event may be unique to one or more systems but, as we have seen, regardless of whether you are monitoring users, modifying users, recovering data, or maintaining the filesystem as a whole, by following a few simple procedures, much of those file, directory, and user-based issues can be solved quickly and efficiently; which leads us gently towards the subject of troubleshooting shared resources.

References

- The Red Hat customer portal: `https://access.redhat.com/documentation/en-US/Red_Hat_Enterprise_Linux/`

- The Tree Project home page: `http://mama.indstate.edu/users/ice/tree/`

- XFS FAQ: `http://xfs.org/index.php/XFS_FAQ`

- The XFS user guide: `http://xfs.org/docs/xfsdocs-xml-dev/XFS_User_Guide//tmp/en-US/html/index.html`

- The Red Hat XFS guide: `https://access.redhat.com/documentation/en-US/Red_Hat_Enterprise_Linux/7/html/Storage_Administration_Guide/ch-xfs.html`

- The XFS wiki page: `http://en.wikipedia.org/wiki/XFS`

6

Troubleshooting Shared Resources

In today's world, the need to share information is pervasive. From the home office to the small office, corporate and enterprise offices to public spaces, maintaining the ability to collaborate information is an important part of fulfilling the role provided by a troubleshooter. Without prejudice, sharing resources or providing access to remote locations is now viewed as an expectation across the spectrum, and it is the purpose of this chapter to discuss and highlight a selection of issues associated with access to shared resources over a network.

In this chapter, we will:

- Discover how to provide NFS shares on a CentOS 7 server
- Learn more about NFS exports
- Learn how to access NFS shared resources on a CentOS 7 client workstation
- Learn how to mount an external drive with CIFS
- Learn how to use `autofs` in order to provide a persistent mount

Providing NFS shares on a CentOS 7 server

NFS shares have been with us for some time and, as in most matters of this type, troubleshooting a file sharing service is fundamentally based on your knowledge of the installation process, as you will spend much of your time reviewing permissions and the network environment, and diagnosing the failure of a service to start.

To begin, you should ensure that both the client workstation and server are able to ping each other:

```
# ping -c 4 XXX.XXX.XXX.XXX
```

If `ping` is successful for both the server and client workstation, to proceed you will need to install the `nfs-utils` package on the server like this:

```
# yum install nfs-utils
```

Having completed the installation, we will now want to create a permanent publication directory in the following way:

```
# mkdir /path/to/nfs/publication/directory
```

For example, one approach is to use the /home directory like this:

```
# mkdir /home/nfs-share
```

As this location is where the client files will be stored, you will want to ensure the privileges are correct by typing:

```
# chmod -R 775 /path/to/nfs/publication/directory
```

> Remember, if you do intend to use the /home directory on the server, be careful when modifying the permissions of the /home directory and target the appropriate subdirectory directly as you will not want to affect any other folders.

The next step is to start the relevant services in the following way:

```
# systemctl enable rpcbind
# systemctl enable nfs-server
# systemctl enable nfs-lock
# systemctl enable nfs-idmap
# systemctl start rpcbind
# systemctl start nfs-server
# systemctl start nfs-lock
# systemctl start nfs-idmap
```

At this point, we will now decide to share the NFS directory over the network by making a few additions to the following file:

```
# nano /etc/exports
```

Where xxx.xxx.xxx.xxx is the IP address of the client workstation, add your network share points in the following way:

```
/path/to/nfs/publication/directory     XXX.XXX.XXX.XXX(rw,sync,root_
squash,no_all_squash)
```

Naturally, you can add as many publication directories as required to one or more users; and each user can have a unique directory based on their IP address. However, if you wish to create a global publication—that is, a single directory that serves all client workstations—then you should use the following syntax:

```
/path/to/nfs/publication/directory     *(rw,sync,no_root_squash,no_all_
squash)
```

Note that a star symbol (*) has replaced the IP address. On a production server or similar, you should avoid this practice and use the network/subnet you are trying to share. This is a particular point for troubleshooters to notice but, for the purpose of explaining the installation procedure, we will use this method for the simple reason that it is a common occurrence.

So, based on our original working example detailed here, the entry could look like this:

```
/home/nfs-share     *(rw,sync,no_root_squash,no_all_squash)
```

Finally, you may need to account for the required firewall changes. To do this, add the following lines one at a time:

```
# firewall-cmd --permanent --zone=public --add-service=nfs
```

```
# firewall-cmd --reload
```

Then restart the NFS service as follows:

```
# systemctl restart nfs-server
```

About NFS exports

At this stage I would like to approach the subject of NFS exports on CentOS 7. As it was noted in the preceding example, we used the following syntax:

```
(rw,sync,root_squash,no_all_squash)
```

Here, most of the options will be obvious to you; root_squash will allow the root user on the client to both access and create files on the NFS server as root. Technically speaking, this option will force NFS to change the client's root to an anonymous ID and, in effect, this will increase security by preventing ownership of the root account on one system migrating to the other system. This is needed if you are hosting root filesystems on the NFS server (especially for diskless clients); with this in mind, it can be used (sparingly) for selected hosts, but you should not use no_root_squash unless you are aware of the consequences.

Other basic options for exports can include:

- no_all_squash: This option disables all squashing.
- rw: This option enables the NFS server to use both read and write requests on a NFS volume.
- ro: This option enables the NFS server to use read-only requests on a NFS volume.
- sync: This option enables the NFS server to reply to requests only after the changes have been committed to stable storage.
- async: This option enables the NFS server to violate the NFS protocol and reply to requests before any changes have been committed to stable storage.
- secure: This option requires that requests originate on an Internet port.
- insecure: This option accepts any or all ports.
- wdelay: This option enables the NFS server to delay committing a write request to a disc if it suspects that another related write request may be in progress or may arrive soon.
- no_wdelay: This option enables the NFS server to allow multiple write requests to be committed to disc within a single operation. This feature can improve performance, but if an NFS server receives many small requests, this behavior can serve to degrade performance. You should be aware that this option has no effect if async is also set.
- subtree_check: This option enables subtree checking.
- no_subtree_check: This option disables subtree checking, which has some implied security issues, but it can improve reliability.
- anonuid=UID: These options explicitly set the uid and gid of the anonymous account; this can be useful when you want all requests to appear as though they are from a single user.
- anongid=GID: This option will disable anonuid=UID.

Mounting NFS shares on a CentOS client

Assuming that your server is currently providing NFS shares, we will now investigate the client workstation in order to ensure that everything is working correctly. This is a task that every troubleshooter needs to know and perfect.

To begin, the client must be using the nfs-utils package like this:

```
# yum install nfs-utils
```

Having completed the installation for the nfs-utils package, you must now create mount points in the following way:

```
# mkdir -p /path/to/mount/point
```

For example, to suit your needs, the preceding command may read as follows:

```
# mkdir -p /mnt/nfs/home
```

Now start the relevant services like this:

```
# systemctl enable rpcbind
# systemctl enable nfs-server
# systemctl enable nfs-lock
# systemctl enable nfs-idmap
# systemctl start rpcbind
# systemctl start nfs-server
# systemctl start nfs-lock
# systemctl start nfs-idmap
```

Finally, we can now mount the NFS share on the client workstation in the following way:

```
# mount -t nfs XXX.XXX.XXX.XXX:/path/to/folder /path/to/mount/point
```

Here, XXX.XXX.XXX.XXX is the IP address of the NFS server and :/path/to/folder is the location of the shared resource. The /path/to/mount/point part represents the location of where the shared resource should be found on the client workstation.

A working example of this command may look like this:

```
# mount -t nfs 192.168.1.100:/home /mnt/nfs/home/
```

In order to confirm that everything is now working, you may want to run the following command:

```
# df -h
```

Based on the working example provided here, the command output should result in showing the addition of one or more filesystems like this:

```
192.168.1.100:/home          21G   33M   21G   1% /mnt/nfs/home
```

Then you can easily confirm the read-write permissions of the NFS resource by creating a new text file in the following way:

```
# touch /path/to/mount/point/nfs-test.txt
```

Using the `ls` command, you should be able to see this file on both the server and the client workstation. However, as this is only a temporary solution, if you decide to make this a permanent or persistent mount, then you should open the following file:

```
# nano /etc/fstab
```

Now add an entry for each mount point, as follows:

```
XXX.XXX.XXX.XXX:/path/to/folder   /path/to/mount/point   nfs defaults
0 0
```

Having completed these steps, you will now be able to reboot the client machine in the full knowledge that the NFS service will be available at all times.

Mounting an external drive with CIFS

Mounting an external drive on a CentOS 7 workstation or server is considered to be a relatively simple procedure and, in many respects, this will be a daily task for a seasoned troubleshooter. However, on some occasions the process itself does give rise to much confusion as to what steps are required and, with this in mind, it is our purpose to provide some much needed clarity.

We will begin by confirming whether `cifs` is installed. To do this, type the following command:

```
# rpm -q cifs-utils
```

CIFS, also known as the Common Internet File System, is a file sharing protocol that enables a standard for remote file access across many filesystems. Based on **Server Message Block (SMB)** and running over TCP/IP, `cifs` provides typical file operations such as open, close, read, write, safe caching, and seek. It supports extended non-filesystem attributes, batch requests, and distributed replicated virtual volumes. However, if the system replies in the following way, you will know that `cifs` is not currently installed:

```
package cifs-utils is not installed
```

To fix this issue, simply type the following command to install the `cifs` package:

```
# yum install cifs-utils
```

At this point, you will need to decide where you want to mount the device, a simple process that can be achieved in the following way:

```
# mkdir /path/to/mount/folder
```

Then use the `cifs-utils` package to mount the external drive by typing:

```
# mount -t cifs //XXX.XXX.XXX.XXX/path/to/folder /path/to/mount/folder
```

However, if you want to pass a string or a series of variables such as a username and password, then the complete command should call the `-o` options like this:

```
# mount -t cifs //XXX.XXX.XXX.XXX/path/to/folder /path/to/mount/folder -o
user=<username> password=<password>
```

It is important to realize that this same process can be used to mount many different types of shared resources, and if the external resource contains spaces in the relevant folder names, then this can be accounted for in the usual way:

```
# mount -t cifs //XXX.XXX.XXX.XXX/path/to/folder\ name /path/to/mount/
folder -o user=<username>,password=<password>
```

The type of string you use can also take advantage of other features that are addressed by the manual. However, the important point to remember is that the preceding solution will only maintain the mounted drive until the drive is unmounted, disconnected, or a reboot occurs. So, nothing at this stage is permanent or persistent.

Using autofs to mount an external drive

If you wish to make the process of attaching an external drive (through `cifs`) permanent (persistent), then you will need to begin by installing the `autofs` package in the following way:

```
# yum install autofs
```

Having installed the package, you will then need to ensure that you start and enable the `autofs` service like this:

```
# systemctl start autofs
# systemctl enable autofs
```

Having done this, and assuming we will be using the same mount point as discussed here, you should begin the configuration of the autofs service by creating a credentials file in your favorite text editor by typing this:

```
# nano /path/to/credentials.txt
```

Now, add the required network credentials like this:

```
username=<access_username>
password=<access_password>
```

Having saved and closed this file, make sure that the permissions are modified to ensure system security:

```
# chmod 600 /path/to/credentials.txt
```

The next stage of this process is to open the autofs configuration file:

```
# nano /etc/auto.master
```

Add the following line at the end of this file, but be sure to customize the values shown here:

```
/path/to/mount/folder   /etc/auto.cifs   --timeout=600 --ghost
```

As you can see, we have used various options, where the --timeout option sets the idle time (in seconds) before unmounting the share if it is not accessed (the default period is 10 minutes). The use of the --ghost option is recommended as it creates a ghost or empty holding folder for the mount point during periods when it isn't mounted.

Now, create and edit the following mount file:

```
# nano /etc/auto.cifs
```

Add and customize the following line to suit your needs:

```
<Local-Name>   -fstype=cifs,rw,noperm,credentials=/path/to/credentials.
txt    ://XXX.XXX.XXX.XXX/path/to/share/folder
```

The Local-Name used will be displayed in the mount point directory (/path/to/mount/point/Local-Name), while the arguments that follow simply call on the filesystem type, irrespective of whether you are providing read-write access and the expected access credentials. So, if you plan to provide read-only access, remember to swap out rw for ro. Moreover, given the structure of the customization made, you can see how multiple locations can be added (this also implies that multiple credentials can be called) in the following way:

```
<Local-Name>   -fstype=cifs,rw,noperm,credentials=/path/to/
credentials1.txt    ://XXX.XXX.XXX.XXX/path/to/share/folder1
<Local-Name>   -fstype=cifs,rw,noperm,credentials=/path/to/
credentials2.txt    ://XXX.XXX.XXX.XXX/path/to/share/folder2
<Local-Name>   -fstype=cifs,rw,noperm,credentials=/path/to/
credentials3.txt    ://XXX.XXX.XXX.XXX/path/to/share/folder3
```

Finally, if you wish to avoid the use of an IP address, then you should ensure that the hostname is mapped to your system via /etc/hosts or DNS in order for you to use the following syntax changes:

```
<Local-Name>   -fstype=cifs,rw,noperm,credentials=/path/to/credentials.
txt    ://hostname/path/to/share/folder
```

Having completed these steps, the next task is to reboot your system but, as an alternative, you can simply restart the autofs service in order to enjoy the benefits of your work:

```
# systemctl restart autofs
```

Summary

In this chapter, we have considered a unique approach to the provision and access of shared resources across a network. From NFS to cifs, fstab to autofs, we have covered the process of making our mounts temporary or permanent and ensured we have argued the case to prove that CentOS can serve all operating systems. However, unlike the other chapters so far, instead of taking the direct approach to diagnosis, we have defined the role of a troubleshooter as a review of the installation process so that your understanding and appreciation of the problems typically associated with shared resources is based on the initial install rather than an event that happens post-installation. In this way, and by knowing the installation procedure, you will also know how to fix any issues associated with that service. With that in mind we will now move on to the subject of troubleshooting security issues.

References

The Red Hat customer portal: https://access.redhat.com/documentation/en-US/Red_Hat_Enterprise_Linux/

7
Troubleshooting Security Issues

In this chapter, we will discuss the issues related to the security of CentOS 7. However, instead of taking a traditional tour relating to hardening a server, we will take a more pragmatic approach by reviewing SSH, SELinux, HIDS, and Firewalld in an alternate fashion in order to encourage you to discover more about the system in general.

In this chapter, we will:

- Discover how to use `aureport` to generate audit reports and audit SELinux with `setroubleshoot`
- Learn how to add and manage SSH banners and use `FIGlet` to create custom banners
- Discover more about the rudiments of tuning the SSH service
- Learn how to install `Tripwire` and provide your system with an intrusion detection system
- Discover more about Firewalld, zone management, and how to add/remove interfaces, ports, and masquerade your infrastructure
- Learn how to remove Firewalld and return to iptables

Auditing SELinux with aureport and setroubleshoot

Disabling SELinux is something that happens quite regularly. It is a common occurrence when hosted control panels are used, or when one or more specific applications seem to be experiencing such difficulties that they will not run with SELinux enabled. In these instances, the act of disabling SELinux is a tried-and-tested technique that can save the system's administrator an immense amount of time. For many, this is an automatic response, while others will argue that the tools associated with SELinux are probably more at home on the desktop, workstation, on servers with a GUI, or in a controlled network environment. However, the fact is simple, the act of disabling SELinux will remove a key component of security and leave the system exposed. I agree, SELinux is a complex system, and for those of us who wish to enjoy the protection it offers, our lives can be made simpler through the option of running aureport like this:

```
# aureport --avc | tail -n 10
```

This will provide a list of avc messages, the output of which may look like this:

```
AVC Report
===========================================================
# date time comm subj syscall class permission obj event
===========================================================
1. 04/18/2015 13:50:53 ? system_u:system_r:init_t:s0 0 (null) (null)
(null) unset 384
2. 04/18/2015 13:55:49 ? system_u:system_r:init_t:s0 0 (null) (null)
(null) unset 789
```

The aureport utility is designed to create column-based reports that show the events recorded in the audit log files, and by taking this one step further, you can also use this same utility to create a list of executable files with the following variation:

```
# aureport -x
```

The output of which, depending on the nature of your system, could look like this:

```
5988. 05/03/2015 12:40:01 /usr/sbin/crond cron ? 0 773
5989. 05/03/2015 12:40:01 /usr/sbin/crond cron ? 0 774
5990. 05/03/2015 12:50:01 /usr/sbin/crond cron ? -1 775
5991. 05/03/2015 12:50:01 /usr/sbin/crond cron ? -1 776
5992. 05/03/2015 12:50:01 /usr/sbin/crond cron ? 0 778
5993. 05/03/2015 12:50:01 /usr/sbin/crond cron ? 0 779
```

```
5994.  05/03/2015 12:50:01 /usr/sbin/crond cron ? 0 780
5995.  05/03/2015 12:50:01 /usr/sbin/crond cron ? 0 781
5996.  05/03/2015 13:00:01 /usr/sbin/crond cron ? -1 782
5997.  05/03/2015 13:00:01 /usr/sbin/crond cron ? -1 783
5998.  05/03/2015 13:00:01 /usr/sbin/crond cron ? 0 785
5999.  05/03/2015 13:00:01 /usr/sbin/crond cron ? 0 786
6000.  05/03/2015 13:00:01 /usr/sbin/crond cron ? 0 787
6001.  05/03/2015 13:00:01 /usr/sbin/crond cron ? 0 788
6002.  05/03/2015 13:01:01 /usr/sbin/crond cron ? -1 789
6003.  05/03/2015 13:01:01 /usr/sbin/crond cron ? -1 790
6004.  05/03/2015 13:01:01 /usr/sbin/crond cron ? 0 792
6005.  05/03/2015 13:01:01 /usr/sbin/crond cron ? 0 793
6006.  05/03/2015 13:01:01 /usr/sbin/crond cron ? 0 794
6007.  05/03/2015 13:01:01 /usr/sbin/crond cron ? 0 795
```

Others may want to use this utility in order to generate a full authentication report by using the following syntax:

```
# aureport -au -i
```

The output of which would look similar to this:

```
Authentication Report
===============================================
# date time acct host term exe success event
===============================================
1. 04/18/2015 12:40:57 root 192.168.1.17 ssh /usr/sbin/sshd yes 343
2. 04/18/2015 12:40:57 root 192.168.1.17 ssh /usr/sbin/sshd yes 346
3. 04/18/2015 19:28:26 root 192.168.1.17 ssh /usr/sbin/sshd yes 1099
4. 04/18/2015 19:28:26 root 192.168.1.17 ssh /usr/sbin/sshd yes 1102
5. 04/19/2015 04:57:06 root 192.168.1.17 ssh /usr/sbin/sshd yes 345
```

To generate a summary report of failed authentication events, use the following command:

```
# aureport -au --summary -i --failed
```

You can create an opposing summary report of successful authentication events with the following syntax:

```
# aureport -au --summary -i --success
```

So, given the depth of reporting at your disposal, when you are dealing with a system that runs SELinux, your first point of call as a troubleshooter is to consider the benefits of aureport when auditing the system. However, as an addition, you will also want to consider a tool called setroubleshoot.

The setroubleshoot tool can be installed with the following syntax:

```
# yum install setroubleshoot setools
```

Having done this, you have now equipped the system with a tool that will actively return announcements from the log file found at /var/log/audit/audit.log and translate them into something far more "human-friendly". This tool is called sealert and its purpose is to issue reports and resolutions regarding any issues related to SELinux.

A process can be started by invoking the following command:

```
# sealert -a /var/log/audit/audit.log
```

However, if you're expecting a large return of data, then the following variation may be more applicable to your needs:

```
# sealert -a /var/log/audit/audit.log | less
```

However, before we exit our discussion on auditing SELinux, for those of you who are running headless and would like to receive e-mail alerts, a final configuration change may be necessary.

To do this, we will open the following file in our favorite text editor:

```
# nano /etc/setroubleshoot/setroubleshoot.conf
```

Scroll down this file to find the [email] section and add your e-mail address to the following line by replacing the relevant text:

```
    from_address = SELinux_Troubleshoot
```

Now, create the relevant list of recipients by customizing the following command:

```
echo "email@domain.com" >> /var/lib/setroubleshoot/email_alert_recipients
```

The setroubleshoot command may not be the perfect solution for everyone and every environment, but the effect of using this package is to realize that regardless of whether you are running a headless server, a server with a GUI, or even a desktop workstation, SELinux Alert is a solution that will enable you to keep using and enjoying the benefits of SELinux without sacrificing your security.

Given the weight of this subject, further reading regarding SELinux and setroubleshoot is available at the end of this chapter.

SSH banners

Using SSH banners is not exactly troubleshooting in its purest form (and yes, we are dipping into the subject of hardening). However, as it is often considered to be a good idea that all servers carry some form of legal banner, notice, or security warning that should be displayed to a user before and after the SSH authentication process is started and finished, it is an area we should explore. Troubleshooters do not build systems, but they do fix them and, for this reason, it is something you will be expected to know. Moreover, as this provides an entry into the world of SSH, learning how to develop your very own (and unique) SSH login banners will be a nice place to start.

To display a banner prior to SSH authentication, you should open the following file in your favorite editor:

```
# nano /etc/issue.net
```

Now, add the desired message, notice, or security notice as required, but remember, try to keep it short and simple.

For example, you may want to say:

```
Warning! You are entering a secure area. This service is restricted
to authorized users only. All activities on this system are logged.
Any unauthorized access will be fully investigated and reported to the
appropriate law enforcement agencies.
```

Having done this and saved the file, you should now open the master configuration file for SSH in your favorite text editor like this:

```
# nano /etc/ssh/sshd_config
```

Then scroll down until you find the following line:

```
#Banner
```

Uncomment it and add the correct path to `issue.net` like this:

```
Banner /etc/issue.net
```

Now save and close the file before restarting the SSH service in the following way:

```
# systemctl restart sshd
```

At this point, you should check the status of the SSH service at any time by typing this:

```
# systemctl status sshd
```

You can qualify the banner settings used by SSH with:

```
# grep -i banner /etc/ssh/sshd_config
```

However, let's say you wanted to provide a unique message by converting plain text to a large ASCII banner.

To do this, we will need to install a small utility called `FIGlet`:

```
# yum install figlet
```

To use `FIGlet`, you simply need to use the following syntax:

```
# figlet "My Message Here"
```

However, for the purposes of our SSH banner, we will want to create a message that is stored on a local file like this:

```
# figlet "My Message Here" > /path/to/banner.txt
```

Having done this, simply return to the following file:

```
# nano /etc/ssh/sshd_config
```

Now find where you previously uncommented this line:

```
    Banner /etc/issue.net
```

Replace the target path with the path to your new banner file created with `FIGlet`:

```
    Banner /path/to/banner.txt
```

To finish, save and close the file, and then restart the SSH service like this:

```
# systemctl restart sshd
```

You could say that was it, but if you wish to provide an additional post-login message, then this can be achieved by editing the following file:

```
# nano /etc/motd
```

Again, simply add the desired message before saving and closing the file in the usual way. After you have completed these steps, the next time a user completes SSH authentication they will not only be greeted by a server message, but they will also be welcomed by a secondary message, thereby giving you plenty of opportunities to provide system users with suitable instruction and reports where required.

Remember, login banners can be useful for two main reasons. They not only provide a small message to users before accessing the system, but also serve to warn against unauthorized access while delivering important information to system administrators without their needing to request it.

Tuning SSH

SSH is the definitive way of communicating with your system. It is a vital service to the lifeblood of your system and it maintains a single, system-wide configuration file that enables the system administrator to modify the operation of the daemon.

SSH access is generally given using the following syntax:

```
# ssh username@ipaddress
```

However, if things are particularly slow, the first step in troubleshooting your system is to use the alternative debug mode like this:

```
# ssh username@ipaddress -vvv
```

So with this in mind, let's take a closer look at this file to assist you in the process of troubleshooting the sshd daemon as a whole.

We will begin by opening the following file in our favorite text editor:

```
# nano /etc/ssh/sshd_config
```

Seen as a good practice when dealing with dictionary attacks, scanners, or bots, you can change the SSH port by simply replacing the value #Port 22 with something completely different, such as Port 2222.

You can also restrict the root login (this is always recommended) by updating the following value to read as follows:

```
    PermitRootLogin no
```

To disable tunneled clear passwords, you should uncomment the following line:

```
    PermitEmptyPasswords no
```

SSH logs can be difficult at times, so before we end this brief review of SSH, if it is felt that the system is going through a stage difficult to diagnose, it is often a good idea to simply uncomment and update the logging parameters like this:

```
    #LogLevel INFO
```

Modify this to read:

```
LogLevel VERBOSE
```

Otherwise, if necessary, higher levels of logging can be achieved with:

```
LogLevel DEBUG
```

Now, the final modification may not prevent an attack, but by requiring SSH to look up, the remote hostname through forward and reverse DNS will generate the appropriate warnings in the system log files. To do this, simply find the following line:

```
#UseDNS yes
```

Update this line to read:

```
UseDNS yes
```

However, if SSH is still acting rather sluggish, then ensuring that SSH does not require a reverse DNS lookup can improve the situation immensely. To do this, simply change the preceding line to read:

```
UseDNS no
```

Moreover, it is also possible that a difficulty may arise from the use of GSSAPI authentication. This is not common as it is a feature of SSH that is called upon when a GSSAPI server is required to validate the relevant user credentials. To avoid this, you should add or edit the following line to read:

```
GSSAPIAuthentication no
```

Further to this, you may also want to consider the subject of timeouts. This common problem can be managed by configuring the correct ServerAliveInterval, ServerAliveCountMax, and TCPKeepAlive values. I have made a simple recommendation here, but you should remember to ensure that these values are appropriate to your needs.

For example, the following rules imply that a packet will be issued every 60 seconds:

```
ServerAliveInterval 15
ServerAliveCountMax 3
TCPKeepAlive yes
```

Adjusting the following values can serve to provide a more sustainable connection:

```
ClientAliveInterval 30
ClientAliveCountMax 5
```

Finally, to make the SSH service just a little bit more secure, scroll down to the bottom of the main configuration file and add the following line in order to maintain a list of usernames that will be allowed to undertake the SSH authentication process:

```
AllowUsers <username1> <username2>
```

Alternatively, instead of enabling access on a per-user basis, this process of managing identities can be simplified on a per-group basis like this:

```
AllowGroup <groupname>
```

Your job is nearly done, but having said all that, and depending on your reasons for troubleshooting the SSH daemon, you must remember to ensure that, when your work is finished, the SSH service must be secured against the possibility of an attack. So, always keep in mind that a successful troubleshooting session will not only fix the problem, it will also serve to ensure the continuation of a safe and secure server.

For example, for those of you who are not using SELinux, fail2ban, or other such security measures, you can always review the login records at any time by typing:

```
# cat /var/log/secure | grep 'sshd'
```

The output of which will look like this:

```
May  3 13:57:24 centos7 sshd[2479]: pam_unix(sshd:session): session
closed for user root
May  3 13:57:28 centos7 sshd[3313]: Accepted password for root from
192.168.1.17 port 51093 ssh2
May  3 13:57:28 centos7 sshd[3313]: pam_unix(sshd:session): session
opened for user root by (uid=0)
```

And, should you wish to view a list of failed attempts, you could try the following:

```
# cat /var/log/secure | grep 'sshd.*Failed'
```

Accepted login attempts can be viewed with:

```
# cat /var/log/secure | grep 'sshd.*Accepted'
```

Intrusion detection with Tripwire

Tripwire is a **host-based intrusion detection system (HIDS)**. It works by collecting configuration and filesystem details and uses this information to provide a reference point between the previous state of a system and its current state, a process that is achieved by monitoring which files or directories were added or modified recently, who changed them, what changes were made, and when the changes took place.

As discussed in a previous chapter, you will need access to the EPEL repository in order to get Tripwire. When you are ready, it can be installed like this:

```
# yum install tripwire
```

To begin using Tripwire, you will need to create the appropriate local and site keys with the following syntax:

```
# tripwire-setup-keyfiles
```

When prompted, add a passphrase for both the site and local key file. Tripwire will advise you to use a combination of uppercase and lowercase letters, digits, and punctuation marks and, when complete, you will be asked to sign the configuration file with the previously created site passphrase.

Once this process is complete, you have the chance to customize Tripwire by making changes to the following file:

```
# nano /etc/tripwire/twpol.txt
```

Before you begin, it is advisable to read through `twpol.txt` as many of the default directories used will not necessarily be available to your system. These extra lines will not cause you any specific problems, but they should be commented out if you want to avoid meaningless error messages.

You can achieve this by commenting the following lines:

```
### Filename: /root/.Xauthority
### No such file or directory
### Continuing...
```

Further to this, you should also spend some time reviewing the following file in order to customize Tripwire for a suitable purpose:

```
# nano /etc/tripwire/twcfg.txt
```

So, having made the relevant changes, you should now update the Tripwire policy file in the following way:

```
# tripwire --update-policy --secure-mode low /etc/tripwire/twpol.txt
```

Tripwire will now step through various onscreen phases to reference your changes; when it has finished, you should now be able to initialize the Tripwire database like this:

```
# tripwire --init
```

Tripwire will now begin to scan the system, but this may take some time depending on the overall size of the system in question:

```
Wrote database file: /var/lib/tripwire/server1.server1.com.twd
The database was successfully generated.
```

When complete, you can run a Tripwire report with the following syntax:

```
# tripwire --check --interactive
```

By running the preceding command, Tripwire will automatically open the report in vi and, from this point onwards, all subsequent reports will be made in the compare mode. So having done this, why not take this opportunity to create a few simple text files or directories in your home folder and rerun the report so that the findings of Tripwire become much more obvious.

Remember, if any changes to the filesystem are considered to be the result of a system intrusion, the administrator will be notified and they will need to restore the system with files and directories that can be trusted. For this reason, any system changes must be validated through Tripwire.

You can validate your current policy file by running the following command:

```
# tripwire --check
```

You can send Tripwire reports via e-mail with utilities such as mutt in the following way:

```
# yum install mutt
```

```
# tripwire --check | mutt -s "Tripwire report" email@domain.com
```

Or by modifying the later part of the daily cron job:

```
# nano /etc/cron.daily/tripwire-check
```

By including the following line:

```
    test -f /etc/tripwire/tw.cfg &&  /usr/sbin/tripwire --check | /bin/
    mail -s "Tripwire File Integrity Report" emailaddress@domain.com
```

Of course, in the space of a few short paragraphs, we have now managed to take a small but significant step towards building a comprehensive host-based intrusion system. It is not troubleshooting in the purest form of the word, but it will help you to diagnose an issue at some point in the future. Moreover, between now and then, you can read more about `Tripwire` by reviewing the manual like this:

```
# man tripwire
```

However, and just before we finish, at this stage, I would suggest that you secure both the `twpol.txt` and `twcfg.txt` files. In the full knowledge that Tripwire's policy file is far more extensible than what has been suggested, in order to assist your ongoing learning I have provided a link to the project home page at the end of this chapter.

Firewalld – zone, service, and port management

The purpose of Firewalld is to replace the need for iptables and improve the management of security by enabling configuration changes without stopping the current connections. Firewalld runs as a daemon that allows for rules to be added and changed instantly and it uses network zones to define a level of trust for any and all associated network connections. For the troubleshooter, this does provide a range of flexible options but, more importantly, it is necessary to understand that, while a connection can only be a part of a single zone, a zone can be used across many network connections.

To know whether Firewalld is currently running, you can type:

```
# firewall-cmd --state
```

To list the predefined zones, you can use:

```
# firewall-cmd --get-zones
```

These zones can be defined as:

- `drop`: In this zone, incoming network packets are dropped (with no reply), and only outgoing network connections are possible
- `block`: In this zone, only network connections initiated within this system are possible as all incoming network connections are rejected with an `icmp-host-prohibited` message
- `public`: This zone is used in areas where you do not trust the other computers; only selected incoming connections are accepted
- `external`: This zone is used on external networks with masquerading enabled and only selected incoming connections are accepted
- `dmz`: This is the demilitarized zone
- `work/home/internal`: This zone is used in environments where you mostly trust the other computers on the network; again, only selected incoming connections are accepted
- `trusted`: In this zone, all network connections are accepted

However, by extending this command, we can also discover what the default zone is by typing:

```
# firewall-cmd --get-default-zone
```

The value of this can be updated with the following syntax:

```
# firewall-cmd --set-default-zone=<new-zone-name>
```

Taking this one step further, we can extend this command to provide not only a list of zones, but also network interface information like this:

```
# firewall-cmd --get-active-zones
```

In this situation, network interfaces can be managed with the following syntax:

```
# firewall-cmd --zone=<zone-name> --add-interface=<device-name>
# firewall-cmd --zone=<zone-name> --change-interface=<device-name>
# firewall-cmd --zone=<zone-name> --remove-interface=<device-name>
```

We can change the assignment of network interfaces and bind them to different zones using the following command:

```
# firewall-cmd --permanent --zone=<zone-name> --change-interface=<device-
name>
```

Finally, you can obtain all the relevant information about any particular zone by typing:

```
# firewall-cmd --zone=<zone-name> --list-all
```

You can list all supported services with:

```
# firewall-cmd --get-services
```

Then you can manage additional services within a zone using the following commands:

```
# firewall-cmd --zone=<zone-name> --add-service=<service-name>
# firewall-cmd --zone=<zone-name> --remove-service=<service-name>
```

Otherwise, list all ports open in any particular zone with this:

```
# firewall-cmd --zone=<zone-name> --list-ports
```

You can manage the addition or removal of TCP/UDP ports like this:

```
# firewall-cmd --zone=<zone-name> --add-port=<port-number/protocol>
# firewall-cmd --zone=<zone-name> --remove-port=<port-number/protocol>
```

Finally, and without trying to over-complicate the array of commands available, you can configure masquerading in the following way:

```
# firewall-cmd --zone=<zone-name> --add-masquerade
# firewall-cmd --zone=<zone-name> --remove-masquerade
```

Then query it like this:

```
# firewall-cmd --zone=<zone-name> --query-masquerade
```

You can manage port forwarding with these commands:

```
# firewall-cmd --zone=<zone-name> --add-forward-port=<port-number>
# firewall-cmd --zone=<zone-name> --remove-forward-port=<port-number>
```

For example, in a typical configuration, if you want to send all packets intended for port 22 to port 2222, you can use the following syntax:

```
# firewall-cmd --zone=external --add-forward-
port=22:proto=tcp:toport=2222
```

So, as you can see, Firewalld is comprehensive, but in the full knowledge that there are many more commands that can be discussed, the intention is to show that a troubleshooter has the ability to dynamically manage firewall architecture without ever needing to stop or restart the firewall service. This is something that cannot be achieved with iptables; in many respects, based on the associated learning curve and the plethora of new commands, it is a defining feature that may prove to be a great success.

Further information about Firewalld can be found at the end of this chapter.

Removing Firewalld and returning to iptables

Firewalld may not be to everyone's liking and you may prefer iptables. So, on a final note, if you ever find yourself in a situation where you do not want to use Firewalld, you can return to iptables easily.

To begin with, you should disable Firewalld like this:

```
# systemctl disable firewalld
# systemctl stop firewalld
```

You should then install and configure iptables by typing:

```
# yum install iptables-services
# touch /etc/sysconfig/iptables
# touch /etc/sysconfig/ip6tables
```

Now, start the iptables service with the following commands:

```
# systemctl start iptables
# systemctl start ip6tables
# systemctl enable iptables
# systemctl enable ip6tables
```

From this point onwards, you now have iptables as your firewall service of choice. However, just before you go, it is probably a good idea to reboot your server in order for the kernel to account for the new configuration.

To do this, type:

```
# reboot
```

Summary

From the more passive positioning of SSH banners and notices to the rigid approach involved in building a host-based intrusion detection system, in this chapter we covered a number of approaches intended to provide a way forward in troubleshooting security. We have not only talked about the release of Firewalld, and how it can be used to dynamically re-engineer the entire firewall environment without an interruption in service, but we have also discussed OpenSSH and shown you the way back to using iptables.

I believe everyone would agree that security is a big subject and its methods and approaches are found throughout the pages in this book. However, having toured this chapter, I hope that this small stepping-stone will serve you well in the future before we take the next step with a discussion on troubleshooting database services.

References

- The Red Hat customer portal: `https://access.redhat.com/documentation/en-US/Red_Hat_Enterprise_Linux/`

- The Fedora project – the SELinux troubleshooting tool (setroubleshoot): `https://fedorahosted.org/setroubleshoot/wiki/SETroubleShoot%20Overview`

- Oracle – configuring and using SELinux: `http://docs.oracle.com/cd/E37670_01/E36387/html/ol_selinux_sec.html`

- The Fedora project – Docs/Drafts/SELinux/SETroubleShoot/DeveloperFAQ: `http://fedoraproject.org/wiki/Docs/Drafts/SELinux/SETroubleShoot/DeveloperFAQ`

- The FIGlet home page: `http://www.figlet.org`

- The Tripwire project home page: `http://sourceforge.net/projects/tripwire/`

- The SSH Wikipedia page: `http://en.wikipedia.org/wiki/Secure_Shell`

- The SSH project home page: `http://www.openssh.com`

- The FirewallD Fedora project: `https://fedoraproject.org/wiki/FirewallD`

- RHEL – using Firewalls: `https://access.redhat.com/documentation/en-US/Red_Hat_Enterprise_Linux/7/html/Security_Guide/sec-Using_Firewalls.html`

8
Troubleshooting Database Services

Database services play a vital role within today's corporate infrastructure, and yet this chapter is not aimed at programmers, database administrators, or developers. Instead, the following pages will take the alternative point of view in order to develop the conversation for system administrators and troubleshooters who are primarily working with CentOS 7. So, let's begin our journey by looking at some of the more common problems associated with databases as a whole in order to provide a troubleshooter's guide to MariaDB, MySQL, and PostgreSQL.

In this chapter, we will:

- Learn how to get up-and-running with MariaDB on CentOS 7
- Learn how to reset and recover a lost password for the root user with MariaDB
- Learn how to tune both MariaDB and MySQL server with `mysqltuner`
- Discover how to run metrics across the MariaDB and MySQL servers
- Learn how to remove MariaDB and return to the MySQL server
- Learn how to install and configure PostgreSQL on CentOS 7

Getting up-and-running with MariaDB

In the latest release of CentOS, you will find that MariaDB has replaced MySQL. It is correct to say that there are similarities between the two database systems, but it is also important to recognize that they are both very different systems. Based on this premise, a typical issue often begins at the point of installation, where the following message may prove to be more than uncomfortable:

```
Redirecting to /bin/systemctl start  mysqld.service.
Failed to issue method call: Unit mysqld.service failed to load: No such
file or directory.
```

In this case, your first action is to verify what is currently installed. This can be achieved by running one or more of the following commands:

```
# which mysql
# ls -la /bin/my*
# ps -ef | grep mysql
```

However, given that the output will seem to be misleading to the untrained eye, this issue provides a point of confusion, and it happens as a result of trying to run the MySQL installation and startup commands. Yes, it is an easy mistake to make, and the most effective means of troubleshooting this issue is to explore the correct way of installing MariaDB.

To install MariaDB, you should use the following command:

```
# yum install mariadb mariadb-server
```

To start the MariaDB service, simply execute the following commands:

```
# systemctl start mariadb.service
# systemctl enable mariadb.service
```

The output of which will result in:

```
ln -s '/usr/lib/systemd/system/mariadb.service' '/etc/systemd/system/
multi-user.target.wants/mariadb.service'
```

To complete the installation, you should now run the following command:

```
# mysql_secure_installation
```

Remember, you have not set a password at this stage. So, when prompted, just press the *return* key to signify that there is no current password and complete the secure installation process by following the prompts as required. As an addition to this, you may also see the following error message:

```
/usr/bin/mysql_secure_installation: line 379: find_mysql_client: command
not found
```

This message can be safely ignored as it represents an outstanding bug associated with Fedora 19 (see the references at the end of this chapter for Red Hat Bugzilla - Bug 1020055).

The complete `mysql_secure_installation` procedure runs as follows:

```
NOTE: RUNNING ALL PARTS OF THIS SCRIPT IS RECOMMENDED FOR ALL MariaDB.
SERVERS IN PRODUCTION USE! PLEASE READ EACH STEP CAREFULLY!


In order to log into MariaDB to secure it, we'll need the current

password for the root user. If you've just installed MariaDB, and

you haven't set the root password yet, the password will be blank,

so you should just press enter here.


Enter current password for root (enter for none): type enter

OK, successfully used password, moving on...


Setting the root password ensures that nobody can log into the MariaDB
root user without the proper authorisation.


Set root password? [Y/n] <Y>

New password: your-password

Re-enter new password: your-password

Password updated successfully!

Reloading privilege tables..

... Success!


By default, a MariaDB installation has an anonymous user, allowing anyone
to log into MariaDB without having to have a user account created for
them. This is intended only for testing, and to make the installation go
a bit smoother. You should remove them before moving into a production
environment.
```

```
Remove anonymous users? [Y/n] <Y>

... Success!


Normally, root should only be allowed to connect from 'localhost'. This
ensures that someone cannot guess at the root password from the network.


Disallow root login remotely? [Y/n] <Y>

... Success!


By default, MariaDB comes with a database named 'test' that anyone can
access. This is also intended only for testing, and should be removed
before moving into a production environment.


Remove test database and access to it? [Y/n] <Y>

 - Dropping test database...

... Success!

 - Removing privileges on test database...

... Success!


Reloading the privilege tables will ensure that all changes made so far
will take effect immediately.


Reload privilege tables now? [Y/n] <Y>

... Success!


Cleaning up...


All done! If you've completed all of the above steps, your MariaDB

installation should now be secure.


Thanks for using MariaDB!
```

From this point on, everything should feel familiar once again and you can begin by checking the status of MariaDB at any time with the following command:

```
# systemctl status mariadb.service
```

Resetting and recovering a root password with MariaDB

The act of resetting a root password provides true currency for a system troubleshooter. It can happen—and yes, it does happen more times than you can imagine—but by following the next few steps, a crisis can be averted.

To begin, you will need to stop the MariaDB service like this:

```
# systemctl stop mariadb.service
```

The next step is to activate "safe mode" in the following way:

```
# mysqld_safe --skip-grant-tables --skip-networking
```

Now run the following sequence to access the MySQL console and connect to the database:

```
# mysql -u root
# use mysql;
```

At this point, we now want to create a new password for the root user, flush the new privileges, and exit the MySQL console like this:

```
# update user set password=PASSWORD("NEW_PASSWORD") where User='root';
# flush privileges;
# exit
```

Having completed these steps, you can either reboot the server or simply stop and start the MariaDB service in the following way:

```
# systemctl stop mariadb.service
# systemctl start mariadb.service
```

Finally, you can now access the database with the new root user credentials by typing:

```
# mysql -u root -p
```

Tuning MariaDB and MySQL

The MYSQL tuner is a useful package that connects to a running instance of your database service and provides a series of configuration recommendations based on the current workload. Naturally, such a tool will not always provide the perfect answer for your system, but you should allow the database system to run for one or more days under a typical workload before introducing a modified configuration.

To install the `mysqltuner` package (part of the EPEL repository), you should type this:

```
# yum install mysqltuner
```

To run the `mysqltuner` package from the command line, you can use the following syntax at any time:

```
# mysqltuner
```

Now, depending on your system configuration and hardware, the output of `mysqltuner` will look similar to this:

```
>>  MySQLTuner 1.2.0 - Major Hayden <major@mhtx.net>
 >>  Bug reports, feature requests, and downloads at http://mysqltuner.
com/
 >>  Run with '--help' for additional options and output filtering
Please enter your MySQL administrative login: <username>
Please enter your MySQL administrative password: <password>


-------- General Statistics -----------------------------------------
[--] Skipped version check for MySQLTuner script
[OK] Currently running supported MySQL version 5.5.41-MariaDB
[OK] Operating on 64-bit architecture


-------- Storage Engine Statistics ----------------------------------
[--] Status: +Archive -BDB +Federated +InnoDB -ISAM -NDBCluster
[--] Data in PERFORMANCE_SCHEMA tables: 0B (Tables: 17)
[!!] InnoDB is enabled but isn't being used
[OK] Total fragmented tables: 0


-------- Security Recommendations  ----------------------------------
[OK] All database users have passwords assigned
```

```
-------- Performance Metrics ------------------------------------
[--] Up for: 1h 35m 23s (33 q [0.006 qps], 15 conn, TX: 16K, RX: 1K)
[--] Reads / Writes: 75% / 25%
[--] Total buffers: 288.0M global + 2.8M per thread (151 max threads)
[OK] Maximum possible memory usage: 708.0M (38% of installed RAM)
[OK] Slow queries: 0% (0/33)
[OK] Highest usage of available connections: 0% (1/151)
[OK] Key buffer size / total MyISAM indexes: 128.0M/99.0K
[!!] Key buffer hit rate: 73.3% (15 cached / 4 reads)
[!!] Query cache is disabled
[OK] Temporary tables created on disk: 0% (0 on disk / 2 total)
[!!] Thread cache is disabled
[OK] Table cache hit rate: 2700% (27 open / 1 opened)
[OK] Open file limit used: 2% (23/1K)
[OK] Table locks acquired immediately: 100% (59 immediate / 59 locks)
[!!] Connections aborted: 6%


-------- Recommendations -----------------------------------------
General recommendations:
    Add skip-innodb to MySQL configuration to disable InnoDB
    MySQL started within last 24 hours - recommendations may be
inaccurate
    Enable the slow query log to troubleshoot bad queries
    Set thread_cache_size to 4 as a starting value
    Your applications are not closing MySQL connections properly
Variables to adjust:
    query_cache_size (>= 8M)
    thread_cache_size (start at 4)
```

The `mysqltuner` package is designed to enable you to make ongoing adjustments to the performance and stability of your MySQL installation. Much of the output is verbose, and it shows you the current configuration variables along with an array of current status data that results in a summary of some general performance recommendations.

It is advisable that you allow the database to run under typical conditions for at least 24 hours before any changes are made. However, should you wish to take advantage of one or more of these recommendations, then you can add them to, or integrate them with, your existing MySQL configuration file:

```
# nano /etc/my.cnf
```

Upon completion, you will be required to restart the database service in question in order to take advantage of the changes made.

You can do this by typing the following command:

```
# systemctl restart mariadb.service
```

Then confirm the database status using this command:

```
# systemctl status mariadb.service
```

The output of which may look similar to this:

```
mariadb.service - MariaDB database server
   Loaded: loaded (/usr/lib/systemd/system/mariadb.service; enabled)
   Active: active (running) since Mon 2015-05-04 07:10:58 EDT; 9s ago
  Process: 4756 ExecStartPost=/usr/libexec/mariadb-wait-ready $MAINPID
(code=exited, status=0/SUCCESS)
  Process: 4726 ExecStartPre=/usr/libexec/mariadb-prepare-db-dir %n
(code=exited, status=0/SUCCESS)
 Main PID: 4755 (mysqld_safe)
   CGroup: /system.slice/mariadb.service
           ├─4755 /bin/sh /usr/bin/mysqld_safe --basedir=/usr
           └─4911 /usr/libexec/mysqld --basedir=/usr --datadir=/var/lib/
mysql --plugin-dir=/usr/lib64/mysql/plugin --log-error=/...


May 04 07:10:56 centos7 systemd[1]: Starting MariaDB database server...
May 04 07:10:56 centos7 mysqld_safe[4755]: 150504 07:10:56 mysqld_safe
Logging to '/var/log/mariadb/mariadb.log'.
May 04 07:10:56 centos7 mysqld_safe[4755]: 150504 07:10:56 mysqld_safe
Starting mysqld daemon with databases from /var/lib/mysql
May 04 07:10:58 centos7 systemd[1]: Started MariaDB database server.
```

Remember, as system requirements and database needs change on an ongoing basis, you can keep running `mysqltuner` as often you like in order to see whether further recommendations have been made.

Obtaining metrics from MariaDB and MySQL

Metrics not only enable you to build a character analysis of your database server, but they can provide evidence of an unexpected behavior. For the troubleshooter, this type of data is important and that can be obtained by running the following command:

```
# mysqladmin -u root -p status
```

The output will provide the following information:

- Uptime: This value represents the number of seconds the database server has been running.
- Threads: This value indicates the number of connected clients.
- Questions: This value indicates the number of queries served since the database server was started.
- Slow queries: This value indicates the number of queries that have exceeded the long_query_time.
- Opens: This value indicates the number of tables that have been served to clients.
- Flush tables: This value indicates the number of flush requests served by the database server. This includes the flush, refresh, and reload commands.
- Open tables: This value indicates the number of tables that are currently open.
- Queries per second avg: This value indicates the number of queries the database server receives per second.

However, as the preceding command is quite slim on detail, greater detail can be obtained by using the following syntax:

```
# mysqladmin -u root -p extended-status
```

An alternative or real-time approach can be obtained by using the following command:

```
# mysqladmin -i 10 -u root -p processlist
```

Note the use of the -i option. This indicates that a 10-second pause will take place before the command will refresh. Based on this, you can establish a real-time monitor of the database server events, thereby enabling you to identify, capture, and kill any queries that can be slowing down the system as a whole.

Returning to MySQL

In some environments, you will want CentOS 7 to use MySQL as opposed to installing MariaDB. To do this, you will need to ensure that MariaDB is not installed, which can be done by running the following command:

```
# yum remove mysql-server mysql-libs mysql-devel mysql*
```

You should now check to confirm whether it has been removed using the following command:

```
# rpm -qa | grep mysql
```

To begin the installation of MySQL, you should download the YUM repository configuration file from `http://dev.mysql.com/downloads/repo/yum/`.

Now, you will not need an account to download this file, but for those of you who do not want to tour the Oracle website, at the time of writing this book it is possible to bypass the preceding process and use the following syntax:

```
# rpm -Uvh http://dev.mysql.com/get/mysql-community-release-el7-5.noarch.rpm
```

You can then run the appropriate installation command like this:

```
# yum install mysql-community-server
```

Ensure that the MySQL daemon is enabled to start on boot by running this command:

```
# systemctl enable mysqld
```

You can now start the server:

```
# systemctl start mysqld
```

Then, run the MySQL secure installation routine in the usual way:

```
# mysql_secure_installation
```

Finally, rerunning the following command will confirm that the process was successful:

```
# ps -ef | grep mysql
```

Installing and configuring PostgreSQL 9

PostgreSQL is fast, robust, cross-platform, and maintains an excellent pedigree. However, in order to troubleshoot when or where an irregular or unexpected event took place, it is always best to begin by remembering how this database service is installed.

To begin this process, we must add the relevant repository in the following way:

```
# rpm -iUvh http://yum.postgresql.org/9.3/redhat/rhel-7-x86_64/pgdg-
centos93-9.3-1.noarch.rpm
```

You should always confirm that you are downloading the appropriate version by visiting the repository itself but, having completed this step, you can now install PostgreSQL like this:

```
# yum install postgresql93-server
```

At this stage, you may want to make some configuration changes to PostgreSQL. To begin, open the following file in your favorite text editor like this:

```
# nano /var/lib/pgsql/9.3/data/postgresql.conf
```

The preceding configuration is verbose, and in most cases, you will be simply uncommenting lines or substituting the relevant values to suit your environment. For example, to make the PostgreSQL database server listen on a specific IP address, you will have to uncomment the following line:

```
#listen_addresses = 'localhost'
```

Then you can change this to suit the IP address of your choice like this:

```
listen_addresses = 'XXX.XXX.XXX.XXX'
```

However, depending on what flavor of Linux you come from, in instances where you may or may not be looking for the `tcpip_socket` parameter, you should use the following syntax instead:

```
listen_addresses = '*'
```

Taking this one step further, you should also spend time making relevant changes to the other settings found within this file. This can include the port used, the maximum number of connections supported, authentication timeout, resource usage, and the many more features afforded by PostgreSQL before opening the following file in order to adjust network access to the database server:

```
# nano /var/lib/pgsql/9.3/data/pg_hba.conf
```

For example, if you want to provide local network access for an entire IP range (for example, 192.168.1.0/24), you can use the following syntax:

```
host all all 192.168.1.0 255.255.255.0 trust
```

Alternatively, for peace of mind, you can use the following syntax to achieve a similar result with slightly less typing:

```
host all all 192.168.1.0/24 md5
```

So, having completed the preceding steps to enable PostgreSQL at boot, you must type:

```
# systemctl enable postgresql-9.3
```

To initialize the database server, you must type this:

```
# /usr/pgsql-9.3/bin/postgresql93-setup initdb
# systemctl start postgresql-9.3
```

Finally, if you want to access the database server, you must switch to the predefined PostgreSQL user account like this:

```
# su - postgres
```

Then you can proceed to connect to the PostgreSQL database in the following way:

```
# psql
```

Then, by using the following expression, you will be able to review the full list of psql commands available to you in order that you can begin adding users and templates, and creating databases:

```
# \?
```

For example, to quit the psql console at any time, use the following syntax:

```
# \q
```

Finally, having returned to the standard bash console, you can confirm PostgreSQL connectivity at any time by customizing the following command:

```
# psql -h <database_hostname> -U <username> -d <database_name>
```

Alternatively, you can use the ps command like this:

```
# ps -ef | grep posgres
```

Summary

From installation and optimization to recovering a lost password for the root user, in this chapter we have highlighted a number of issues related to the process of troubleshooting both MariaDB and PostgreSQL. As was stated at the outset, there was no intention to deal with specific programming or development issues, but as these database systems can be found throughout the enterprise, it is expected that you will be dealing with them; in this respect, we have discussed a range of topics that will provide a useful starting point when troubleshooting almost any database service.

In the next chapter, we will further the theme of the book and discuss a unique approach to troubleshooting web services.

References

- The MySQL project home page: `http://dev.mysql.com/`
- MySQL YUM downloads: `http://dev.mysql.com/downloads/repo/yum/`
- The MariaDB project home page: `https://mariadb.org/en/`
- MariaDB FAQ: `https://mariadb.com/kb/en/mariadb/faq/`
- Installing MariaDB with Yum: `https://mariadb.com/kb/en/mariadb/yum/`
- Red Hat Bugzilla – Bug 1020055, `https://bugzilla.redhat.com/show_bug.cgi?id=1020055`
- The MySQLTuner home page: `http://mysqltuner.com`
- The MySQLTuner GitHub home page: `https://github.com/major/MySQLTuner-perl`
- Benchmarking MariaDB-5.3.4: `https://blog.mariadb.org/benchmarking-mariadb-5-3-4/`
- Troubleshooting problems – starting the MySQL server: `http://dev.mysql.com/doc/refman/5.1/en/starting-server.html`
- MariaDB versus MySQL – compatibility: `https://mariadb.com/kb/en/mariadb/mariadb-vs-mysql-compatibility/`
- PostgreSQL 9.3.6 documentation: `http://www.postgresql.org/docs/9.3/static/index.html`
- PostgreSQL client authentication: `http://www.postgresql.org/docs/9.3/static/client-authentication.html`
- PostgreSQL database roles: `http://www.postgresql.org/docs/9.3/static/user-manag.html`
- PostgreSQL repositories: `http://yum.postgresql.org/repopackages.php`

9
Troubleshooting Web Services

Troubleshooting is not always about disaster recovery or fixing broken systems. In fact, most troubleshooters tend to spend their time discovering ways to constantly improve a system or assisting other colleagues to get the best out of the technology at hand. Some would call this Dev/Ops, but regardless of how you look at it, the essential principles remain the same. You are a troubleshooter, and you are a crucial part of the support network; so with this in mind, we will take a break from "saving the day" and approach the subject of web services a little more proactively.

In this chapter, we will review the subject of investigating web services with the purpose of making improvements and to build on your knowledge as a troubleshooter.

In this chapter, we will:

- Learn how to audit the server with cURL
- Discover ways to check your Akamai headers
- Learn how to implement Varnish on Apache
- Discover how to validate your Varnish installation with cURL
- Learn how to use cURL in order to access an FTP directory
- Learn how to monitor Apache by installing `mod_status`

Auditing the server with cURL

When a web server begins to exhibit problems, it can be for a vast number of reasons. However, when experiencing the issue as a troubleshooter, remember that you are not looking at the application itself (this is the realm of programmers and they will not thank you for joining in), but you will be looking at the state of the server.

Essentially, you can say that this is a process to scrutinize the server and its ability to serve web pages or web applications. So, let's begin by checking to confirm that cURL is installed.

To do this, you should use the following syntax:

```
# yum install curl
```

Having completed this step, you are now ready to run your first cURL command:

```
$ curl http://www.example.com
```

More specifically, you can choose a particular location in the following way:

```
$ curl http://www.example.com/path/to/homepage.html
```

Alternatively, you can pass a string like this:

```
$ curl http://www.example.com/path/to/homepage.html?query=string
```

Each of the preceding commands will show the entire HTTP content of the target URL; and yes, it can make the screen look a bit messy. Thus, instead, you can invoke the tidy option like this:

```
$ curl http://www.example.com | tidy -i
```

However, if you wish to capture data and save the output to a file of your choice, then you can achieve this by using the command-line redirection method like this:

```
$ curl http://www.example.com > /path/to/folder/example.html
```

Alternatively, you can use the -o option in the following way:

```
$ curl -o /path/to/folder/example.txt http://www.example.com
```

Note that by invoking the -o option approach, the target file must be stated first. However, given that the preceding example shows that we are saving the output to a text file, you can quite happily change this to almost any type of file you want, like this:

```
$ curl -o /path/to/folder/example.html http://www.example.com
```

Now, working on the assumption that network connectivity is good, we have chosen cURL because we are now dealing with the specific problem of a web server that may be exhibiting difficulties in displaying web pages.

As we have already seen, by default, cURL will simply output the contents of the web page that was requested. However, by using an assortment of additional options (or arguments), you can extend its abilities and request far more details.

For example, if we use the -w option (write-out), you can obtain the status code of any web page by using the following syntax:

```
$ curl -w "%{http_code}\n %{content_type}\n" http://www.example.com/path/
to/page.html
```

Here, \n is used to output the result on a new line (you can also output a tab with \t or a carriage return with \r). You should now know the HTTP status code and HTTP content type for the web page in question.

For example, you can try this:

```
$ curl -w "%{http_code}\n %{content_type}\n" https://www.packtpub.com/
virtualization-and-cloud/troubleshooting-centos
```

The result of the preceding command is a bit too extensive to print in full, but at the end of the output, you should see the following (in which the target data is placed on separate lines as requested):

```
    </body>
</html>
200
 text/html; charset=utf-8
```

Moreover, you can even include a remote IP address like this:

```
$ curl -w "%{remote_ip}\n %{http_code}\n %{content_type}\n" http://www.
example.com/path/to/page.html
```

The output of this command should show something like the following towards the end:

```
    </body>
</html>
23.205.169.129
 200
 text/html;charset=UTF-8
```

You can obtain the size (in bytes) of a web page with the following command:

```
$ curl -w "%{size_download}\n" http://www.example.com/path/to/page.html
```

The result of this command will show 63175 bytes towards the end of the output:

```
  </body>
</html>
63175
```

On the other hand, if you are dealing with a web server that uses both 301 and 302 redirection methods, we can use the -L option like this:

```
$ curl -Lw "%{remote_ip}\n %{http_code}\n %{content_type}\n" http://www.
example.com/
```

Finally, if you would like to ensure your investigation of the server's web pages provides a complete list of all the headers cURL may encounter, you should invoke the -v option for verbosity in the following way:

```
$ curl -v http://www.example.com
```

For example, once again you can test Red Hat like this:

```
$ curl -v http://www.redhat.com
```

The result of this command will provide the following output:

```
* About to connect() to www.redhat.com port 80 (#0)
*   Trying 104.66.92.228...
* Connected to www.redhat.com (104.66.92.228) port 80 (#0)
> GET / HTTP/1.1
> User-Agent: curl/7.29.0
> Host: www.redhat.com
> Accept: */*
>
< HTTP/1.1 301 Moved Permanently
< Content-Type: text/html; charset=iso-8859-1
< Location: http://www.redhat.com/en
< Server: Apache
< Content-Length: 296
< Expires: Mon, 04 May 2015 14:53:10 GMT
< Cache-Control: max-age=0, no-cache
< Pragma: no-cache
```

```
< Date: Mon, 04 May 2015 14:53:10 GMT

< Connection: keep-alive

< Set-Cookie: AWSELB=014101F31CE28463C273156EDFEB4013EF4DC7B4B58B2D05871
92FCB8DB58F8B0E7B8A652EC4DCB07BB3CC9D65387BA7D24617BF645CEBCF6476050FABB
DF5D9227C0A5A30;PATH=/;MAX-AGE=30

<

<!DOCTYPE HTML PUBLIC "-//IETF//DTD HTML 2.0//EN">

<html><head>

<title>301 Moved Permanently</title>

</head><body>

<h1>Moved Permanently</h1>

<p>The document has moved <a href="http://www.redhat.com/en">here</a>.</
p>

<hr>

<address>Apache Server at www.redhat.com Port 80</address>

</body></html>

* Connection #0 to host www.redhat.com left intact
```

While for those of you who would prefer to minimize the output to response headers only, instead of using the preceding command you should invoke the `-I` option like this:

```
$ curl -I http://www.example.com
```

For example, if you retried Red Hat like this:

```
$ curl -I http://www.redhat.com
```

The result of this command will provide the following output:

```
HTTP/1.1 301 Moved Permanently

Content-Type: text/html; charset=iso-8859-1

Location: http://www.redhat.com/en

Server: Apache

Content-Length: 0

Expires: Mon, 04 May 2015 14:55:54 GMT

Cache-Control: max-age=0, no-cache

Pragma: no-cache

Date: Mon, 04 May 2015 14:55:54 GMT

Connection: keep-alive
```

```
Set-Cookie: AWSELB=014101F31CE28463C273156EDFEB4013EF4DC7B4B53E1B0B83C0D
272B9D220605DDE604A12C4DCB07BB3CC9D65387BA7D24617BF642030376EDB73D2D8C226
E62350AE4B75;PATH=/;MAX-AGE=30
```

At this stage, there is always a lot more that can be said about cURL. In fact, you could write an entire book on the subject; however, before we stray too far from our main topic, you will be happy to know that you can discover more about cURL by reading the manual:

```
$ man curl
```

Debugging Akamai headers with cURL

CDNs are becoming commonplace, and the most popular of them all is Akamai. However, where a CDN can deliver benefits, they can also provide a stumbling block when you are troubleshooting a web service, application, or even a simple home page. Look at it this way, with a CDN of any type, you are generally working with cached objects and you want to validate the traffic behavior. So, with this in mind, we will now discuss how cURL can come to the rescue:

To begin with, we must issue a properly formed Pragma header and, to do this, you can use the following syntax:

```
$ curl -IXGET http://www.example.com/path/to/home.html
```

However, if you wish to include the debug information, you can use:

```
$ curl -IXGET -H "Pragma: akamai-x-cache-on, akamai-x-cache-remote-on,
akamai-x-check-cacheable, akamai-x-get-cache-key, akamai-x-get-extracted-
values, akamai-x-get-nonces, akamai-x-get-ssl-client-session-id, akamai-
x-get-true-cache-key, akamai-x-serial-no" http://www.example.com/path/to/
home.html
```

For example, as Red Hat are known users of Akamai, if you try:

```
$ curl -IXGET -H "Pragma: akamai-x-cache-on, akamai-x-cache-remote-on,
akamai-x-check-cacheable, akamai-x-get-cache-key, akamai-x-get-extracted-
values, akamai-x-get-nonces, akamai-x-get-ssl-client-session-id, akamai-
x-get-true-cache-key, akamai-x-serial-no" http://www.redhat.com/en
```

Then, unless there have been any significant changes since the publication of this book (and web pages always do change over time), the output will look similar to this:

```
HTTP/1.1 200 OK
```

```
Content-Language: en
```

```
Content-Type: text/html; charset=utf-8
```

```
ETag: "1430747458-1"

Last-Modified: Mon, 04 May 2015 13:50:58 GMT

Link: <http://www.redhat.com/en>; rel="canonical"

Server: Apache

X-Drupal-Cache: HIT

X-Powered-By: PHP/5.3.3

X-RedHat-Debug: 1

X-Check-Cacheable: NO

Expires: Mon, 04 May 2015 13:51:17 GMT

Cache-Control: max-age=0, no-cache

Pragma: no-cache

Date: Mon, 04 May 2015 13:51:17 GMT

Transfer-Encoding:  chunked

X-Cache: TCP_MISS from a2-20-133-122.deploy.akamaitechnologies.com
(AkamaiGHost/7.2.0-15182023) (-)

X-Cache-Key: /L/1890/356403/3d/www.rollover.redhat.com.akadns.net/en
cid=__

X-True-Cache-Key: /L/www.rollover.redhat.com.akadns.net/en cid=__

X-Akamai-Session-Info: name=CRS_VERSION; value=2.2.6

X-Akamai-Session-Info: name=DC_FORWARD_IP; value=54.187.212.127; full_
location_id=X-DC-Origin-IP

X-Akamai-Session-Info: name=HEADER_NAMES; value=User-
Agent%3aHost%3aAccept%3aPragma; full_location_id=

X-Akamai-Session-Info: name=INITORIGINIP; value=54.187.212.127

X-Akamai-Session-Info: name=NL_2580_BLACKLIST_NAME; value=Black List

X-Akamai-Session-Info: name=NL_6042_ORACLE_NAME; value=Oracle bot-block
(per Keith Watkins by Sri Sankaran)

X-Akamai-Session-Info: name=NSCPCODE; value=298900

X-Akamai-Session-Info: name=OVERRIDE_HTTPS_IE_CACHE_BUST; value=all

X-Akamai-Session-Info: name=PARENT_SETTING; value=TD

X-Akamai-Session-Info: name=SITESHIELDMAP; value=s187.akamaiedge.net

X-Akamai-Session-Info: name=SQLI_SELECT_STATEMENT_COUNT; value=0

X-Akamai-Session-Info: name=SRTOPATH; value=/s/global.css

X-Akamai-Session-Info: name=SS4PMAP; value=www.redhat.com

X-Akamai-Session-Info: name=WAF_CREATE_ASSERTION_EXPIRE_TIME;
value=1430747537

X-Akamai-Session-Info: name=WAF_CRS_ALLOWED_HTTP_VERSIONS; value=HTTP/0.9
HTTP/1.0 HTTP/1.1
```

X-Akamai-Session-Info: name=WAF_CRS_ALLOWED_METHODS; value=GET HEAD POST OPTIONS

X-Akamai-Session-Info: name=WAF_CRS_ARG_LENGTH; value=64000

X-Akamai-Session-Info: name=WAF_CRS_ARG_NAME_LENGTH; value=256

X-Akamai-Session-Info: name=WAF_CRS_CMD_INJECTION_ANOMALY_RULE_TUPLE; value=

X-Akamai-Session-Info: name=WAF_CRS_CMD_INJECTION_ANOMALY_SCORE; value=0

X-Akamai-Session-Info: name=WAF_CRS_CMD_INJECTION_ANOMALY_SCR; value=

X-Akamai-Session-Info: name=WAF_CRS_CRITICAL_ANOMALY_SCORE; value=5

X-Akamai-Session-Info: name=WAF_CRS_DEFAULT_ACTION; value=alert

X-Akamai-Session-Info: name=WAF_CRS_ERROR_ANOMALY_SCORE; value=4

X-Akamai-Session-Info: name=WAF_CRS_INBOUND_ANOMALY_RULE_SCR; value=

X-Akamai-Session-Info: name=WAF_CRS_INBOUND_ANOMALY_RULE_TUPLE; value=

X-Akamai-Session-Info: name=WAF_CRS_INBOUND_ANOMALY_SCORE; value=0

X-Akamai-Session-Info: name=WAF_CRS_INBOUND_MSG; value=

X-Akamai-Session-Info: name=WAF_CRS_INFO_ANOMALY_SCORE; value=1

X-Akamai-Session-Info: name=WAF_CRS_INVALID_HTTP_RULE_TUPLE; value=

X-Akamai-Session-Info: name=WAF_CRS_INVALID_HTTP_SCORE; value=0

X-Akamai-Session-Info: name=WAF_CRS_INVALID_HTTP_SCR; value=

X-Akamai-Session-Info: name=WAF_CRS_MAX_NUM_ARGS; value=255

X-Akamai-Session-Info: name=WAF_CRS_NOTICE_ANOMALY_SCORE; value=2

X-Akamai-Session-Info: name=WAF_CRS_OUTBOUND_ANOMALY_RULE_SCR; value=

X-Akamai-Session-Info: name=WAF_CRS_OUTBOUND_ANOMALY_RULE_TUPLE; value=

X-Akamai-Session-Info: name=WAF_CRS_OUTBOUND_ANOMALY_SCORE; value=0

X-Akamai-Session-Info: name=WAF_CRS_PHP_INJECTION_RULE_SCR; value=

X-Akamai-Session-Info: name=WAF_CRS_PHP_INJECTION_RULE_TUPLE; value=

X-Akamai-Session-Info: name=WAF_CRS_PHP_INJECTION_SCORE; value=0

X-Akamai-Session-Info: name=WAF_CRS_RESTRICTED_EXTENSIONS; value=asa asax ascx backup bak bat cdx cer cfg cmd com config conf cs csproj csr dat db dbf dll dos htr htw ida idc idq inc ini key licx lnk log mdb old pass pdb pol printer pwd resources resx sql sys vb vbs vbproj vsdisco webinfo xsd xsx

X-Akamai-Session-Info: name=WAF_CRS_RESTRICTED_HEADERS; value=Proxy-Connection Lock-Token Content-Range Translate Via If

X-Akamai-Session-Info: name=WAF_CRS_RFI_ANOMALY_RULE_SCR; value=

X-Akamai-Session-Info: name=WAF_CRS_RFI_ANOMALY_RULE_TUPLE; value=

X-Akamai-Session-Info: name=WAF_CRS_RFI_ANOMALY_SCORE; value=0

X-Akamai-Session-Info: name=WAF_CRS_RISK_GROUPS; value=

```
X-Akamai-Session-Info: name=WAF_CRS_RISK_SCRS; value=

X-Akamai-Session-Info: name=WAF_CRS_RISK_TUPLES; value=

X-Akamai-Session-Info: name=WAF_CRS_SQL_INJECTION_RULE_TUPLE; value=

X-Akamai-Session-Info: name=WAF_CRS_SQL_INJECTION_SCORE; value=

X-Akamai-Session-Info: name=WAF_CRS_SQL_INJECTION_SCR; value=

X-Akamai-Session-Info: name=WAF_CRS_TOTAL_ANOMALY_SCORE; value=0

X-Akamai-Session-Info: name=WAF_CRS_TOTAL_ARG_LENGTH; value=64000

X-Akamai-Session-Info: name=WAF_CRS_TROJAN_RULE_SCR; value=

X-Akamai-Session-Info: name=WAF_CRS_TROJAN_RULE_TUPLE; value=

X-Akamai-Session-Info: name=WAF_CRS_TROJAN_SCORE; value=0

X-Akamai-Session-Info: name=WAF_CRS_WARNING_ANOMALY_SCORE; value=3

X-Akamai-Session-Info: name=WAF_CRS_XSS_RULE_SCR; value=

X-Akamai-Session-Info: name=WAF_CRS_XSS_RULE_TUPLE; value=

X-Akamai-Session-Info: name=WAF_CRS_XSS_SCORE; value=0

X-Akamai-Session-Info: name=WAF_DATA_HEADER_SIGN_VAL; value=HnWuQRcXIUfMG
G3LF/9PllRcUxUkocv8aFiFmuExQZE=

X-Akamai-Session-Info: name=WAF_DATA_HEADER_VAL; value=/en 1430747537

X-Akamai-Session-Info: name=WAF_HA_STATUS; value=checking

X-Akamai-Session-Info: name=WAF_MYSQLI_COUNT; value=0

X-Serial: 1890

Connection: keep-alive

Connection: Transfer-Encoding

Set-Cookie: WL_DCID=origin-www-c; expires=Mon, 04-May-2015 21:51:17 GMT;
path=/

Set-Cookie: AWSELB=7DE7FB19045D425DE69229FBB7F229663FD24433135E354B67BC
8404E265E1F485365E31B3F24C3F30EB76C3348446159423E486323BDC9105B0C92244
E19C46091861E2C5;PATH=/;MAX-AGE=30

Set-Cookie: AWSELB=014101F31CE28463C273156EDFEB4013EF4DC7B4B5224485501216
1AA58C6EBAB965CAFA77C4DCB07BB3CC9D65387BA7D24617BF645CEBCF6476050FABBDF5D
9227C0A5A30;PATH=/;MAX-AGE=30

X-Cache-Remote: TCP_MISS from a195-10-11-245.deploy.akamaitechnologies.
com (AkamaiGHost/7.2.0-15182023) (-)
```

Quite a long example I agree, but Akamai headers are quite extensive. Of course, this process is not restricted to web pages per se, as it can be used to target any object of your choice.

For example, if you want to target a particular image, you can use:

```
$ curl -IXGET -H "Pragma: akamai-x-cache-on, akamai-x-cache-remote-on,
akamai-x-check-cacheable, akamai-x-get-cache-key,
akamai-x-get-extracted-values, akamai-x-get-nonces,
akamai-x-get-ssl-client-session-id, akamai-x-get-true-cache-key,
akamai-x-serial-no" http://www.example.com/path/to/image.jpg
```

Alternatively, you can target a CSS file like this:

```
$ curl -IXGET -H "Pragma: akamai-x-cache-on, akamai-x-cache-remote-on,
akamai-x-check-cacheable, akamai-x-get-cache-key,
akamai-x-get-extracted-values, akamai-x-get-nonces,
akamai-x-get-ssl-client-session-id, akamai-x-get-true-cache-key,
akamai-x-serial-no" http://www.example.com/path/to/style.css
```

At this point, I am assuming that you know most of the HTTP response codes (if not, you can find a reference link at the end of this chapter), but before we close this subject, let's take a brief look at some of the less obvious headers you will encounter:

- X-Check-Cacheable: This value will tell us whether the object in question is cacheable by Akamai.

- X-Cache-Key: Ignoring the first two values and starting from the third value in the resulting string, you will see the CP code and the relevant TTL, although the TTL may differ slightly when set at the application level through the Edge-Control header.

- X-Cache: This value will tell us what the Akamai Edge server returned as output. However, this value will also indicate one of the following instances:

  - TCP_HIT: This value implies that the object was fresh in cache and the object was fetched from the disk cache.

  - TCP_MISS: This value implies that the object was not in cache; the server fetched the object from the origin.

  - TCP_REFRESH_HIT: This value implies that the object was stale in cache and we successfully refreshed the origin on an If-Modified-Since request.

  - TCP_REFRESH_MISS: This value implies that the object was stale in cache, and refresh obtained a new object from the origin in response to our If-Modified-Since request.

  - TCP_REFRESH_FAIL_HIT: This value implies that the object was stale in cache, and we failed on refresh (couldn't reach the origin), so we served the stale object.

  - TCP_IMS_HIT: This value implies that an If-Modified-Since request from the client and object was fresh in cache and served.

- ○ `TCP_NEGATIVE_HIT`: This value implies that the object previously returned a "not found" message (or any other negatively cacheable response) and that the cached response was a hit for this new request.

- ○ `TCP_MEM_HIT`: This value implies that the object was on disk and in the memory cache. The server served it without hitting the disk.

- ○ `TCP_DENIED`: This value implies that you have been denied access to the client for whatever reason.

- ○ `TCP_COOKIE_DENY`: This value implies that you have been denied access on cookie authentication (if the centralized or decentralized authorization feature is being used in configuration).

So, as you can see, debugging Akamai headers using cURL is very easy to do. Yes, there are browser plugins that will do the same job, but knowing how to do it with cURL is far more fun.

Adding Varnish to Apache

Varnish is a high-performance HTTP accelerator that not only assists in reducing the overall server load, but also serves to improve website response times. For this reason, it has become very popular; as a consequence of this, we will look at the process of setting up Varnish in conjunction with the Apache web server.

Before we begin, it will be assumed that Apache is installed. Moreover, you should be aware that completing the next steps requires access to the EPEL repository. Please refer to *Chapter 4, Troubleshooting Package Management and System Upgrades*, for instructions on how to download and install the EPEL repository on CentOS 7.

So when you are ready, let's begin by installing Varnish:

```
# yum install varnish
```

Following a successful installation of Varnish, we will need to enable the service at boot. This can be achieved by typing:

```
# systemctl enable varnish
```

We will then need to activate the service like this:

```
# systemctl start varnish
```

So, having completed the basic installation, you can now check the status of Varnish by typing:

```
# systemctl status varnish
```

Then you check what version you are running by typing:

```
# varnishd -V
```

At this stage, we need to complete the basic configuration of this service and enable it to work in conjunction with Apache. To do this, we will begin by opening the main Apache configuration with your favorite text editor like this:

```
# nano /etc/httpd/conf/httpd.conf
```

Now, scroll down to find the following line:

```
Listen 80
```

Replace it with the following line:

```
Listen 127.0.0.1:8080
```

If the web server is running one or more virtual hosts, you will need to make the following adjustment in order to reflect the new port that Apache is listening on:

```
<VirtualHost *:8080>
```

Now save the file and run the following command to check your syntax:

```
# httpd -t
```

The output should read:

```
Syntax OK
```

Now, having completed these steps, we will make our first configuration change to the original Varnish installation:

```
# nano /etc/varnish/varnish.params
```

Scroll down and look for the following line:

```
VARNISH_LISTEN_PORT=6081
```

Replace it with the following:

```
VARNISH_LISTEN_PORT=80
```

Now scroll down and locate the following line:

```
VARNISH_STORAGE=
```

This is where Varnish gets interesting, and where you, as the troubleshooter, get to determine the most suitable method for optimizing web performance. Currently, you will notice that Varnish is configured to use the server's hard disk to cache files, and, in this instance, you have two options.

In a situation where a large cache is expected, where RAM is limited, or you intend to build a dedicated Varnish store to cache files, by making a simple adjustment to reflect the default settings you can specify the size of your cache.

For example, if you want to create a disk cache of 20 GB, you can use the following line:

```
VARNISH_STORAGE="file,/var/lib/varnish/varnish_storage.bin,20G"
```

However, if you want the ultimate Varnish experience that uses a RAM-caching approach, this can be achieved by customizing the following line to reflect the system's needs:

```
VARNISH_STORAGE="malloc,1G"
```

Now let's take this one stage further.

For example, if you want the RAM to cache up to 4 GB of data, you can use:

```
VARNISH_STORAGE="malloc,4G"
```

Alternatively, if you want to improve the performance of a not-so-rich RAM-based environment, you can change this value to 512 MB like this:

```
VARNISH_STORAGE="malloc,512m"
```

You can now save and close this file before opening the following:

 # nano /etc/varnish/default.vcl

This file is the overall configuration file for Varnish. I will not go into the exact details at this point, as there are many Varnish-based books that cover this topic in an exhaustive manner. However, for the purpose of troubleshooting, you will need to make a few basic changes in order to get things up-and-running. To do this, simply ensure that the following section reflects the criteria of the system in question:

```
vcl 4.0;
# Default backend definition. Set this to point to your content
server.
backend default {
    .host = "127.0.0.1";
    .port = "8080";
}
```

Having done this, you should now restart Apache in the following way:

```
# systemctl restart httpd.service
```

Follow this by restarting Varnish like this:

```
# systemctl restart varnish.service
```

Well done! The installation of Varnish is now complete; you can continue to visit your Apache-based websites in the usual manner, but with the added advantage of experiencing improved speed and performance.

Testing Varnish with cURL

If the web server relies on Varnish, then it is particularly important to ensure that your web pages are being cached and that they are served in a timely manner.

To confirm this, you can begin with the following syntax:

```
# curl -I http://www.example.com/index.html
```

Having used the `-I` option to display the headers only, if Varnish is installed, you should see something like this:

```
HTTP/1.1 200 OK
Date: Fri, 06 Mar 2015 00:59:24 GMT
Server: Apache/2.4.6 (CentOS) PHP/5.5.22
X-Powered-By: PHP/5.5.22
Content-Type: text/html; charset=UTF-8
X-Varnish: 5 3
Age: 16
Via: 1.1 varnish-v4
Content-Length: 97422
Connection: keep-alive
```

In the preceding example, the most important lines are the following:

```
X-Varnish: 5 3
Age: 16
```

Now, let's run through a quick explanation of these values:

- X-Varnish: XXXXXXXX XXXXXXXX: The X-Varnish header not only contains an ID of the current request, but also maintains the ID of the request that populated the cache. If there is only one number, you should be aware that the cache was populated with the current request and can be considered to be what is termed a cache miss.

- Age: XXXX: This value indicates how long the content has been stored in cache. If a zero (0) is shown, then it implies that the page in question was not cached at all.

Of course, the exact values shown may be different, but having seen this example, you are now able to not only confirm and verify the functionality of Varnish on your server, but also keep a constant eye on the Age value given (you will know how long (in seconds) a page will exist in the cache).

Using cURL to access an FTP directory

With practice, everyone can use an FTP client, but a situation where you need to script certain events is where you will call on cURL to do all the hard work.

So, by starting at the most basic level, the easiest way to access an FTP directory with an existing username and password will be as follows:

```
$ curl ftp://exampleftpsite.com -u <username>
```

When requested, simply enter your password at the prompt:

```
$ curl ftp://exampleftpsite.com  -u <username>
Enter host password for user '<username>':
```

Now, if you want to search an FTP directory for a particular list of files, you can use the -s silent option and grep in combination like this:

```
$ curl ftp://exampleftpsite.com -u <username> -s | grep <keyword>
```

You can complete your search and upload a file with the following command:

```
$ curl -T filename.zip ftp://exampleftpsite.com -u <username>
```

Or you can make a direct download with the following syntax:

```
$ curl ftp://exampleftpsite.com -u <username> -o filename.zip
```

Again, you should enter the correct password when prompted but, having found the relevant file, you can use the following syntax to discover your current location:

```
$ pwd
```

Finally, to bring this section to an end, you can delete a file in the following way:

```
$ curl ftp://exampleftpsite.com -X 'DELE filename.zip' -u <username>
```

Remember that you need to be extra careful when deleting a file as there will be no prompts. The action to delete with cURL is automatic.

Enabling mod_status in Apache

The mod_status is an Apache module that assists in the practice of monitoring web server load and current httpd connections. It comes complete with an HTML interface, and it is accessible using any browser.

To use mod_status, we need to make a few basic configuration changes to the VirtualHosts file, so let's start at the beginning by creating a rudimentary virtual host with the following command:

```
# nano  /etc/httpd/conf.d/vhost.conf
```

Add the following lines:

```
<VirtualHost *:80>
    DocumentRoot /var/www/html
    ServerName servername.domain.com
</VirtualHost>
```

Remember: if you are using Varnish, ensure that it uses the correct port:

```
<VirtualHost *:8080>
    DocumentRoot /var/www/html
    ServerName servername.domain.com
</VirtualHost>
```

Having done this, you can now add the following lines between the appropriate <VirtualHost></VirtualHost> directives in order to enable mod_status:

```
<Location /server-status>
  SetHandler server-status
  Order allow,deny
  Allow from all
</Location>
```

The end result should look something like this:

```
<VirtualHost *:8080>
    DocumentRoot /var/www/html
    ServerName servername.domain.com

  <Location /server-status>
    SetHandler server-status
    Order allow,deny
    Allow from all
  </Location>
</VirtualHost>
```

You can see the line that reads `Allow from all`. For the purpose of the preceding example, this is fine, but for security reasons, you should lock the connection access to a specific IP address.

For this reason, a better option will be to use the following syntax:

```
<Location /server-status>
  SetHandler server-status
  Order deny, allow
  Deny from all
  Allow from localhost
</Location>
```

Of course, you should customize the preceding example code to suit the needs of your system; when you are finished, simply save and close the file before restarting Apache:

 # systemctl restart httpd

Now, open a browser and visit the chosen virtual host using the following format:

`http://XXX.XXX.XXX.XXX/server-status`

This will give you full access to the static `server-status` page. However, if you append the URL with the `refresh` option as follows, the page should refresh every 5 seconds:

`http://XXX.XXX.XXX.XXX/server-status/?refresh=5`

The resulting page will then show you an array of information that includes server uptime, server load, the total number of connections, CPU usage, process IDs, the total number of requests, and which requests are currently being processed. All of this should prove most useful when you are attempting to highlight any issues related to a specific website on the Apache web server.

Summary

The purpose of this chapter was to take a very different view on troubleshooting web services. From auditing the server with cURL to making performance enhancements with Varnish, we have not only considered the needs of a systems administrator, but we have also discovered the world of CDNs and Dev/Ops with the intention of showing just how versatile a troubleshooter can be and just how important your skills will become.

In the next chapter, we will discuss some techniques used when troubleshooting DNS-based services.

References

- The Wikipedia home page for Curl: `http://en.wikipedia.org/wiki/CURL`
- The Curl home page: `http://curl.haxx.se`
- The Wikipedia home page for HTTP status codes: `http://en.wikipedia.org/wiki/List_of_HTTP_status_codes`
- HTTPie, a curl alternative: `https://github.com/jakubroztocil/httpie`
- The Varnish home page: `https://www.varnish-cache.org`
- Varnish Administrator Documentation: `https://www.varnish-cache.org/docs/trunk/index.html`

10
Troubleshooting DNS Services

As the Domain Name System (DNS) is probably the most influential technology in the world of IT, at some point in your career you should expect that it will be presented to you as an ongoing issue that needs to be managed and resolved. DNS servers come in various forms, and your level of control may vary depending on the type of infrastructure you have access to but, regardless of this, the issues will undoubtedly remain the same, in whole or part.

Having already reviewed the virtue of dig and the various other networking tools, in the final few pages of this book we will now discuss the process of troubleshooting CentOS 7 with specific regard to monitoring issues related to DNS as a function of the overall system health check.

In this chapter, we will:

- Learn how to change the hostname of the system using hostnamectl and managing the fqdn with /etc/hosts
- Learn how to perform a few basic system and BIND-based sanity checks before hitting the panic button
- Learn how to monitor bandwidth with iftop
- Learn how to flush the cache

Changing the hostname and managing the FQDN

Changing the hostname of an authoritative or a recursive (caching) server may not necessarily be a DNS issue (per se), but, as a rule of thumb, the hostname of your system is inextricably linked to the DNS as a function of the overall system in question; for this reason, we will now review the procedure to change the hostname of the host system.

To review the current hostname, you can use the following syntax:

```
# hostnamectl status
```

However, you can choose to view the static, transient, or pretty name with one of the following commands:

```
# hostnamectl status --static
# hostnamectl status --transient
# hostnamectl status --pretty
```

Based on this, to change the hostname you should use the following command:

```
# hostnamectl set-hostname <new-host-name>
```

Alternatively, you can choose to update the static hostname with this:

```
# hostnamectl --static set-hostname <new-host-name>
```

Having completed this action, the hostname change will be applied to the kernel automatically without any need to reboot. Subsequently, any change to the hostname must be reflected in the system's networking configuration.

To do this, you will have to check and confirm /etc/hosts is up-to-date by typing:

```
# nano /etc/hosts
```

A typical post-installation (or default) file will look like this:

```
127.0.0.1    localhost localhost.localdomain localhost4 localhost4.
localdomain4
::1          localhost localhost.localdomain localhost6 localhost6.
localdomain6
```

To proceed, simply change the file to read as follows by substituting the relevant values that suit your system configuration:

```
127.0.0.1     localhost localhost.localdomain localhost4 localhost4.
localdomain4
```

```
192.168.1.183    <servername>.<domain-name>.<tld> <server-name>
::1              localhost localhost.localdomain localhost6 localhost6.
localdomain6
```

For example, if your server name is `centos7` (hostname) and it is on the `centos.local` domain, then your file will look like this:

```
127.0.0.1        localhost localhost.localdomain localhost4 localhost4.
localdomain4
192.168.1.200    centos7.centos.local centos7
::1              localhost localhost.localdomain localhost6 localhost6.
localdomain6
```

Once this is complete, you can confirm the hostname by typing this:

 # hostname

Then you can confirm and print the current FQDN by typing the following command:

 # hostname -f

However, if you discover that the new hostname has not been accepted or updated, then simply type the following command to resolve any outstanding issues:

 # systemctl restart systemd-hostnamed

You can then confirm these changes by running `ping` on the server in the following way:

 # ping -c 4 <hostname>

Based on the preceding example, if you run:

 # ping -c 4 centos

The output of `ping` should now show the FQDN like this:

```
PING centos7.centos.local (192.168.1.200) 56(84) bytes of data.
64 bytes from centos7.centos.local (192.168.1.183): icmp_seq=1 ttl=64
time=0.048 ms
64 bytes from centos7.centos.local (192.168.1.183): icmp_seq=2 ttl=64
time=0.057 ms
64 bytes from centos7.centos.local (192.168.1.183): icmp_seq=3 ttl=64
time=0.038 ms
64 bytes from centos7.centos.local (192.168.1.183): icmp_seq=4 ttl=64
time=0.094 ms
```

Performing system sanity checks with BIND

DNS failures can be the result of some fairly innocuous issues that arise due to fundamental configuration flaws or recent changes (and updates) to a system. This type of event can happen and, for this reason, it is always useful to run through a checklist of sanity checks before you hit the panic button.

So, by starting with a basic tool such as `ping`, `nslookup`, or `dig`, you can begin testing for areas of concern. For example, you can use `telnet` like this:

```
# telnet <remote-server-address> 53
```

The `telnet` command is a nice and easy tool to use, and if the connection is refused or takes too long, then you can rule out the possibility of RDNS errors by simply renaming the reverse DNS file and trying again.

Now, if you do this, make sure that the forward DNS remains functional and reattempts a telnet connection. If this works, you will know that the RDNS is at fault and you can double-check this by confirming the forward zones with `nslookup`:

```
# nslookup <remote-server-address>
```

However, if you are still unable to connect, then you should restore the RDNS file, check your firewall configuration (and `SELinux`, if used), and then use the following command to view the current status of port 53:

```
# netstat -tulpn | grep :53
```

If you are still encountering difficulties, then you should also check the log files like this:

```
# tail -f /var/log/messages
```

Now confirm the status of the named service:

```
# ps ax | grep named
```

However, it is far more informative if you use the following code:

```
# systemctl status named
```

The output of this command may begin with the following notice before listing any current resolving errors:

```
named.service - Berkeley Internet Name Domain (DNS)
   Loaded: loaded (/usr/lib/systemd/system/named.service; disabled)
   Active: active (running) since Sun 2015-05-03 07:55:14 EDT; 16s ago
  Process: 2853 ExecStart=/usr/sbin/named -u named $OPTIONS (code=exited,
status=0/SUCCESS)
  Process: 2851 ExecStartPre=/usr/sbin/named-checkconf -z /etc/named.conf
(code=exited, status=0/SUCCESS)
 Main PID: 2855 (named)
   CGroup: /system.slice/named.service
   └─2855 /usr/sbin/named -u named


May 03 07:55:15 centos7 named[2855]: error (network unreachable)
resolving 'pdns196.ultradns.info/AAAA/IN': 2001:500:49::1#53

May 03 07:55:15 centos7 named[2855]: error (network unreachable)
resolving 'pdns196.ultradns.info/A/IN': 2001:500:1b::1#53

May 03 07:55:15 centos7 named[2855]: error (network unreachable)
resolving 'pdns196.ultradns.info/AAAA/IN': 2001:500:1b::1#53

May 03 07:55:15 centos7 named[2855]: error (network unreachable)
resolving 'ns1.isc.ultradns.net/AAAA/IN': 2610:a1:1014::e8#53

May 03 08:55:15 centos7 named[2855]: error (network unreachable)
resolving './DNSKEY/IN': 2001:7fd::1#53

May 03 08:55:15 centos7 named[2855]: error (network unreachable)
resolving './NS/IN': 2001:7fd::1#53

May 03 08:55:15 centos7 named[2855]: error (network unreachable)
resolving './DNSKEY/IN': 2001:dc3::35#53

May 03 08:55:15 centos7 named[2855]: error (network unreachable)
resolving './NS/IN': 2001:dc3::35#53
```

If all is well, the next step will be to check your zone files for errors:

```
# named-checkconf /etc/named.conf
```

Remember, if no errors are found, then no output will be provided. However, if you do encounter an error, depending on the system in question, the output may look like this:

```
/etc/named.conf:106: missing ';' before 'zone'
```

Moving beyond this, you can also use the provided package called `named-checkzone` to check and confirm the overall integrity and syntax of a zone file. It works by creating a false load situation and thereby runs the same validation rules as it would before it is loaded into the system. In this way, it makes a remarkably reliable approach to confirming new zone files before adding them to a production server.

To use `named-checkzone`, you have to type:

```
# named-checkzone localhost /var/named/<filename>
```

Alternatively, you can check a specific hostname with:

```
# named-checkzone <hostname> /var/named/<filename>
```

On the other hand, if you are in a situation where no nameserver is currently configured or the nameserver is found to be inaccessible, the first port of call is to check the system's resolver in order to confirm that it is configured correctly by opening the following file:

```
# nano /etc/resolv.conf
```

Having opened this file, you will notice that the first entry should point to the primary or master nameserver followed by an entry for the secondary or slave nameserver. Generally speaking, you should expect to see at least two nameservers, but three is also common. Depending on the system's configuration, an example of `/etc/resolv.conf` may look like this:

```
search local
    nameserver XXX.XXX.XXX.XXX
    nameserver XXX.XXX.XXX.XXX
```

For example, if you were using Google's DNS, then the primary nameserver will be 8.8.8.8 and the secondary nameserver will be 8.8.4.4. Consequently, your file will look like this:

```
search local
    nameserver 8.8.8.8
    nameserver 8.8.4.4
```

On the off chance that the system is using `127.0.0.1` or `localhost` as the primary or sole nameserver, then you should also expect to find forwarders being used in the main DNS configuration file. The exact nature of how this is to be done will depend on what DNS application you are currently using. However, in the case of `BIND`, this would be found within the `options` section of `/etc/named.conf` as follows:

```
forwarders {
XXX.XXX.XXX.XXX;
XXX.XXX.XXX.XXX;
};
```

Moreover, while you are reviewing the `BIND` configuration file, you should also ensure that recursion is disabled in order to reduce recursive queries, and thereby protect the system from the risk of `DDoS Amplication` attacks like this:

```
allow-transfer    { 127.0.0.1; XXX.XXX.XXX.XXX; };
recursion no;
```

Now, confirm that BIND is actually listening on port 53:

```
listen-on port 53 { 127.0.0.1; XXX.XXX.XXX.XXX; };
```

Remember, when you are testing DNS, you should ensure that port 53 is open on both UDP and TCP ports. This is because UDP queries larger than 512 bytes can be truncated and TCP is used as a failover solution. So, remember to check the firewall configuration in order to see whether you need to make any required changes; and if you do, remember to restart the firewall.

Having done this, you can then check the current status of `BIND` by typing this:

```
# systemctl status named
```

Then, start or stop the service as required by using one or more of the following system commands:

```
# systemctl start named
```
```
# systemctl restart named
```
```
# systemctl stop named
```

Following this, and based on the assumption that the zone files are not only correct (including the forward and reverse zones), but also maintain the correct permissions, you should also check `/etc/hosts` in order to confirm that the appropriate configuration is available to the system.

To do this, open /etc/hosts in your favorite text editor like this:

```
# nano /etc/hosts
```

An example of this file looks like this:

```
127.0.0.1         localhost.localdomain localhost
XXX.XXX.XXX.XXX   <servername>.<domainname>.<tld>   <servername>
::1               localhost6.localdomain6 localhost6
```

If you need to add any specific or dedicated IP address to the host file, then simply add them underneath the first three lines like this:

```
127.0.0.1         localhost.localdomain localhost
XXX.XXX.XXX.XXX   <servername>.<domainname>.<tld>   <servername>
::1               localhost6.localdomain6 localhost6


XXX.XXX.XXX.XXX        live.intranet.local
XXX.XXX.XXX.XXX        staging.intranet.local
XXX.XXX.XXX.XXX        production.intranet.local
```

Finally, you should also check and confirm the configuration for your Ethernet device, which can be accessed by opening the relevant Ethernet connection at /etc/sysconfig/network-scripts. As you can see, this configuration file often indicates a preference for a specific Gateway, DNS, and Domain setting. In this respect, ensuring that these settings are accurate can be seen as good practice.

As shown here, based on the previous example, the output of cat /etc/sysconfig/network-scripts/ifcfg-eth0 may look like this:

```
TYPE=Ethernet
BOOTPROTO=none
DEFROUTE=yes
IPV4_FAILURE_FATAL=no
IPV6INIT=yes
IPV6_AUTOCONF=yes
IPV6_DEFROUTE=yes
IPV6_FAILURE_FATAL=no
NAME=eth0
UUID=30420474-a7c9-4ea1-97b2-17f3b3a104cc
ONBOOT=yes
HWADDR=00:1C:42:1F:E6:BA
IPADDR0= XXX.XXX.XXX.XXX
```

```
PREFIX0= XXX.XXX.XXX.XXX
GATEWAY0= XXX.XXX.XXX.XXX
DNS1= XXX.XXX.XXX.XXX
DNS2= XXX.XXX.XXX.XXX
DOMAIN=local
IPV6_PEERDNS=yes
IPV6_PEERROUTES=yes
```

In this example, it is important to remember that the DNS entries must be added if the system uses the CentOS Network Manager. Moreover, as this only shows a single Ethernet interface, if the system in question has multiple NICs, then do make sure that this checklist includes the additional Ethernet configuration files.

Finally, if you do make any network changes, run the following command to ensure the new settings take effect:

```
# systemctl restart network
```

Now, where xxx.xxx.xxx.xxx is the IP address of the nameserver in question, having run through these basic sanity checks, you should be able to perform or reconfirm your system's configuration by running a successful nslookup request like this:

```
# nslookup www.google.com XXX.XXX.XXX.XXX
```

Alternatively, you can use dig in the following way:

```
# dig www.google.com XXX.XXX.XXX.XXX
```

So, having checked the key components of the system and made sure that the firewall is not blocking any important UDP and TCP traffic, you should be confident that any nonrecursive issues or warnings reported at this stage will (more than likely) be based on a specific configuration issue related to the DNS application itself.

Monitoring bandwidth with iftop

A poorly configured or troublesome DNS server can result in a variety of issues that includes the failure of application servers and an overall network slowdown. However, before we dive into the inner workings of DNS, it is important to realize that network slowdowns can be attributed to various causes; and with this in mind, it is often a good idea to refer to a package known as iftop.

As discussed in a previous chapter, you will notice that iftop is similar to the top command, but unlike the top command, you will discover that its purpose is to remain specifically interested in measuring the bandwidth of network connections between the host server and an external reference point (IP address).

To install this package, you will need the EPEL repository and, after you have enabled this repository by reading the instructions from a previous chapter, iftop can be installed with the following command:

```
# yum install iftop
```

Running the basic package needs no arguments. In fact, a typical iftop session can be started with the following command:

```
# iftop
```

Otherwise, on servers with multiple Ethernet interfaces, where X is the name assigned to your Ethernet interface, you can use the following argument to display the results for a specific device:

```
# iftop -i ethX
```

By default, iftop will attempt to resolve all IP addresses into hostname, but you can avoid this with the -n option like this:

```
# iftop -n -i ethX
```

Moreover, given that the default display is used to show the overall bandwidth between hosts, a useful feature is to swap this display to show the ports that each host is using for communication purposes. To do this, simply use the *P* key during an iftop session to toggle between displaying all ports and the standard bandwidth readouts.

Other useful keyboard shortcuts include:
- Use the *T* key to toggle between display types
- Use the *Shift + P* key to pause a current display
- Use the *J* and *K* keys to scroll the display

As the display screen is relatively verbose and self-explanatory, I will not detail the package itself. However, in certain situations, you should be aware that you can use iftop to investigate the flow of packets across a network range by initializing the appropriate filter like this:

```
# iftop -F 192.168.1.0/255.255.255.0 -i eth0
```

You can choose to show the results for a specific port with the following syntax:

```
# iftop -i eth0 -f 'port http'
```

Alternatively, rather than displaying the results in bits per second, using the -B option in the following way the display will now show bandwidth rates in bytes per second:

```
# iftop -B -F 192.168.1.0/255.255.255.0 -i eth0
```

Remember, the art of troubleshooting is based on the ability to identify the cause as quickly as possible. It is true that network slowdowns can be caused by misconfigured or troublesome DNS issues, but it is also true to say that DNS can be wrongly accused and that such issues can be the result of bandwidth. So, by using this small, but incredibly useful package, you may have saved yourself a lot of time and effort and made a permanent fix to what was previously assumed to be a DNS issue.

You can learn more about iftop by typing:

```
# man iftop
```

Flushing the cache

The Time to Live (TTL) factor can also have a bearing on the issues at hand. In instances where a simple dig request will show that the nameserver displays a different record to the local DNS, then (beyond waiting for the automated update to take place) a different course of action is to flush the cache.

In the case of BIND, it is simply a matter of restarting the service like this:

```
# systemctl restart named
```

However, without being so drastic, you can also use the following syntax:

```
# rndc flush
```

Then run a service status check:

```
# systemctl status named
```

In this respect, you should now see the following notices:

```
received control channel command 'flush'
flushing caches in all views succeeded
```

Alternatively, you can target a specific domain with the following syntax:

```
# rndc flushname google.com
```

And, having run the `systemctl status named` command, you will see the following reports:

```
received control channel command 'flushname google.com'
flushing name 'google.com' in all cache views succeeded
```

Now, in the case of propagating immediate changes to local desktop clients, you will need to close all running applications, and then follow one of these procedures.

For Windows users, simply open Command Prompt and use:

```
# ipconfig /flushdns
```

For Mac OS-X 10.10, open Terminal and use the following command:

```
# sudo discoveryutil udnsflushcaches
```

For Mac OS-X 10.5.2 to 10.6, use the following command:

```
# dscacheutil -flushcache
```

For older versions of OS-X, use this:

```
# lookupd -flushcache
```

Summary

The purpose of this chapter was not necessarily to tackle the issues associated with DNS configuration, as there are many books that deal with this subject comprehensively. However, it was engendered to approach the subject of DNS in relation to it being a function of the services available on a network. The consequence of this was to illustrate a few basic techniques associated with the art of troubleshooting an authoritative or caching domain nameserver that may be exhibiting difficulties during the performance of its role.

So, from changing the hostname to checking the bandwidth, flushing the cache to running some standard sanity checks, you should be aware that troubleshooting is not always about installing and configuring packages. In many respects, very few professional troubleshooters will find themselves building a system from scratch, but they will be asked to fix an apparent issue that, in the context of this book, is typically something more immediate, if not intrinsic to the network environment as a whole.

References

- The Red Hat customer portal: `https://access.redhat.com/documentation/en-US/Red_Hat_Enterprise_Linux/`

- The iftop Wikipedia home page: `http://en.wikipedia.org/wiki/Iftop`

- The Domain Name System Security Extensions Wikipedia home page: `http://en.wikipedia.org/wiki/Domain_Name_System_Security_Extensions`

- The BIND project home page: `https://www.isc.org/downloads/bind/`

- The BIND Wikipedia home page: `http://en.wikipedia.org/wiki/BIND`

- The RHEL customer portal – Chapter 19: `https://access.redhat.com/documentation/en-US/Red_Hat_Enterprise_Linux/5/html/Deployment_Guide/ch-bind.html`

Index

W

web services, troubleshooting
  about 131
  Akamai headers, debugging
     with cURL 136-141
  FTP directory, accessing
     with cURL 145, 146
  mod_status, enabling in Apache 146, 147
  server, auditing with cURL 132-135
  Varnish, adding to Apache 141-144
  Varnish, testing with cURL 144

X

X-Cache
  about 140
  TCP_COOKIE_DENY 141
  TCP_DENIED 141
  TCP_HIT 140
  TCP_IMS_HIT 140
  TCP_MEM_HIT 141
  TCP_MISS 140
  TCP_NEGATIVE_HIT 141

  TCP_REFRESH_FAIL_HIT 140
  TCP_REFRESH_HIT 140
  TCP_REFRESH_MISS 140
X-Cache-Key 140
X-Check-Cacheable 140
XFS filesystem
  extending 80
  fragmentation, investigating 83, 84
  repairs, running 81, 82
  working with 79, 80
X-Varnish 145

Y

Yellowdog Updater 55
Yum
  about 57
  additional repositories, installing 60
  operations, fixing 60
  plugins, using 57-59
Yum repositories
  EPEL 60, 61
  IUS repository 62
  Remi 61

Thank you for buying
Troubleshooting CentOS

About Packt Publishing

Packt, pronounced 'packed', published its first book, *Mastering phpMyAdmin for Effective MySQL Management*, in April 2004, and subsequently continued to specialize in publishing highly focused books on specific technologies and solutions.

Our books and publications share the experiences of your fellow IT professionals in adapting and customizing today's systems, applications, and frameworks. Our solution-based books give you the knowledge and power to customize the software and technologies you're using to get the job done. Packt books are more specific and less general than the IT books you have seen in the past. Our unique business model allows us to bring you more focused information, giving you more of what you need to know, and less of what you don't.

Packt is a modern yet unique publishing company that focuses on producing quality, cutting-edge books for communities of developers, administrators, and newbies alike. For more information, please visit our website at www.packtpub.com.

About Packt Open Source

In 2010, Packt launched two new brands, Packt Open Source and Packt Enterprise, in order to continue its focus on specialization. This book is part of the Packt Open Source brand, home to books published on software built around open source licenses, and offering information to anybody from advanced developers to budding web designers. The Open Source brand also runs Packt's Open Source Royalty Scheme, by which Packt gives a royalty to each open source project about whose software a book is sold.

Writing for Packt

We welcome all inquiries from people who are interested in authoring. Book proposals should be sent to author@packtpub.com. If your book idea is still at an early stage and you would like to discuss it first before writing a formal book proposal, then please contact us; one of our commissioning editors will get in touch with you.

We're not just looking for published authors; if you have strong technical skills but no writing experience, our experienced editors can help you develop a writing career, or simply get some additional reward for your expertise.

Troubleshooting PostgreSQL

ISBN: 978-1-78355-531-4   Paperback: 164 pages

Intercept problems and challenges typically faced by PostgreSQL database administrators with the best troubleshooting techniques

1. Detect and solve performance, indexing, and fuzzy matches problems and more in an effective way.

2. Tune PostgreSQL databases and remove bottlenecks such as low performance queries, failed database connections, and transaction locks that slow down the systems.

3. Hands-on guide with valuable troubleshooting solutions for PostgreSQL database administrators.

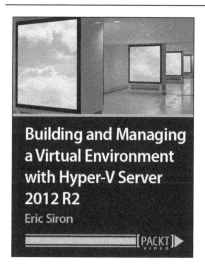

Building and Managing a Virtual Environment with Hyper-V Server 2012 R2

ISBN: 978-1-78217-698-5   Duration: 03:30 hours

Build, deploy, and manage Hyper-V in failover cluster environments

1. Configure node computers for participation in a Hyper-V cluster.

2. Tackle the complicated subjects of storage and networking in a Hyper-V cluster.

3. Maximize uptime for the services provided by your virtual machines.

Please check **www.PacktPub.com** for information on our titles